One with God

ONE WITH GOD

Salvation as Deification and Justification

Veli-Matti Kärkkäinen

LITURGICAL PRESS
Collegeville, Minnesota

www.litpress.org

A title of the Unitas Books series published by the Liturgical Press

Other titles available in the Unitas Books series:

Justification and the Future of the Ecumenical Movement: The Joint Declaration on the Doctrine of Justification
William G. Rusch, ed.

I Believe, Despite Everything: Reflections of an Ecumenist
Jean-Marie R. Tillard

Visible Church—Visible Unity: Ecumenical Ecclesiology and "The Great Tradition of the Church"
Ola Tjørhom

Cover design by McCormick Creative.

ISBN 13: 978-0-8146-2971-0
ISBN 10: 0-8146-2971-7

	4	5	6	7	8

Library of Congress Cataloging-in-Publication Data

Kärkkäinen, Veli-Matti.
    One with God : salvation as deification and justification / Veli-Matti Kärkkäinen.
        p. cm.—(Unitas books)
    Includes bibliographical references and index.
    ISBN 0-8146-2971-7 (pbk : alk. paper)
    1. Justification (Christian theology) 2. Salvation—Lutheran Church.
3. Deification (Christianity) 4. Salvation—Orthodox Eastern Church.
5. Mystical union. 6. Lutheran Church—Relations—Orthodox Eastern
Church. 7. Orthodox Eastern Church—Relations—Lutheran Church.
I. Title. II. Series.

BT764.3.K57   2004
234—dc22

                                                            2004010434

Unitas Books

On the eve of his crucifixion, Jesus prayed that his followers "All may be one" (John 17:21). Christians believe that this promise is fulfilled in the church. The church is Christ's Body and his Body cannot be divided. And yet, the churches today live in contradiction to that promise. Churches that recognize in another Christian community an embodiment of the one church of Jesus Christ still too often find that they cannot live in true communion with them. This contradiction between the church's unity and its division has driven the ecumenical movement over the last century.

The pursuit of unity will require more than a few mutual adjustments among the churches. Ecumenism must involve true conversion, a conversion both of hearts and minds, of the will and the intellect. We all must learn to think in new ways about the teachings and practices of the church. Division has become deeply embedded in the everyday life and thought of the churches. Thinking beyond division will require a new outlook.

Unitas Books seeks to serve the rethinking that is a necessary part of the ecumenical movement. Some books in the series will directly address important topics of ecumenical discussion; others will chart and analyze the ecumenical movement itself. All will be concerned with the church's unity. Their authors will be ecumenical experts from a variety of Christian traditions, but the books will be written for a wider audience of interested clergy and laypersons. We hope they will be informative for the expert and the newcomer alike.

The unity we seek will be a gift of the Holy Spirit. The Spirit works through means, however, and one of the Spirit's means is careful theological reflection and articulate communication. We hope that this series may be used by the Spirit so that the unity won by Christ may be more fully visible "so that the world may believe" (John 17:21).

Norman A. Hjelm
Michael Root
William G. Rusch

The series editor responsible for this volume is Norman A. Hjelm.

v

Contents

Preface

While writing this book, I have more than once consoled my soul with the wise counsel of the leading American Lutheran scholar and ecumenist Robert W. Jenson. At the end of his celebrated treatise on the Trinity, he takes comfort in the confession: "Finally, the very great historical and reflective range that I have tried to cover means that I know less than I need to at some places; without spending my life on this book, that could not be fully rectified."[1]

While academic inquiry usually advances through a rigorous analysis of a limited topic, there is also value in a broader approach such as that of the present book, in which I have tried to take stock of a number of differing perspectives that bear on the topic of salvation. The main goal of the present study—to move toward an ecumenically fruitful convergence regarding the doctrines of salvation of the Eastern and Western wings of the church as well as of the two dominant approaches within the Western churches (Roman Catholic and Lutheran/Protestant)—by definition makes the inquiry broad and entails a look at a number of contributions from the areas of biblical, historical, systematic, and ecumenical studies.

The limitations of this approach are obvious. No single topic can be exhaustively treated, and I fear specialists in each particular field—say, in New Testament or historical studies—will quickly notice that a novice has entered their field. Unless a group of specialists from various fields collaborate, however, limitations of this kind can hardly be overcome.

[1]Robert W. Jenson, *The Triune Identity: God According to the Gospel* (Philadelphia: Fortress, 1982) xiii.

These preliminary reflections are not meant to be apologies; no author should apologize for a new contribution. They are meant, rather, to guide readers to recognize at the outset the kind of goal the author had in mind while producing the study. If this book inspires ecumenical and systematic reflection on the doctrine of salvation within and between Christian churches, its ultimate goal has been more than achieved. The modest constructive proposal in the last chapter is meant both to outline my current understanding of convergences between Eastern Orthodox, Roman Catholic, and Protestant (both Lutheran and so-called Free Churches) soteriologies and to point to urgent tasks of further inquiry. Having simultaneously been at work on two books dealing with a Christian theology of religions, I am also enthused about the implications of the present project for relations with other religions.

Several persons deserve a big thank you. Norman A. Hjelm saw potential in this project and was instrumental in placing this work in the new and ambitious ecumenical series, Unitas Books of which he is an editor. Michael Root, another editor of the series, worked closely with me in revising the text. Another recent book in this series, *Justification and the Future of the Ecumenical Movement: The Joint Declaration on the Doctrine of Justification,* which was edited by the third editor of Unitas Books, William G. Rusch,[2] while released too late to be consulted for this book, and even though its focus is much more limited, in a wonderful way complements my own approach in that it represents a group of specialists writing on the topic of justification.

My theological mentor and *Doktorvater* Professor Emeritus Tuomo Mannermaa of the University of Helsinki and his younger colleagues first introduced me during my doctoral studies to the new developments in both Lutheran and Orthodox soteriology. My acquaintance with Catholic theology was strengthened through a year-long stay at St. John's University and the Institute for Ecumenical and Cultural Research, Collegeville, Minnesota, under the mentorship of Fr. Kilian McDonnell, O.S.B.; to its most hospitable staff, I owe heartfelt thanks (Liturgical Press has its home in the very same Benedictine abbey and university).

Years of experience in ecumenical meetings, consultations, and working groups in the World Council of Churches, the Faith and Order movement, and international bilateral dialogues have given me many opportunities to learn from others across the ecumenical spectrum.

---

[2]William G. Rusch, ed. *Justification and the Future of the Ecumenical Movement: The Joint Declaration on the Doctrine of Justification* (Collegeville, Liturgical Press, 2003).

Presentations on the topic in academic conferences, most recently at the Eastern Orthodox Study Group of the American Academy of Religion Annual Meeting in Atlanta, in November 2003, have exposed me to the constructive critique of academic colleagues.

I am, finally, grateful to Susan Carson Wood, the faculty publications specialist for the School of Theology at Fuller Theological Seminary, who helped yet another book of this author for whom English is not a mother tongue see light in a form that more closely follows the idioms of this continent.

Veli-Martti Kärkkäinen
Fuller Theological Seminary
Pasadena, California
Lent 2004

Abbreviations

EKD   Evangelical Church in Germany
FC   Formula of Concord
HDT   *Heidelberg Disputation*
LW   *Luther's Works,* American Edition. Jaroslav Pelikan and Helmut
      Lehmann, eds. St. Louis: Concordia and Philadelphia: Fortress
      Press; 55 vols.
MESJ Publications of the Finnish Society for Ecumenics and Missiology
PG   Patrologia graeca
WA   *Weimarer Ausgabe* (the standard abbreviation for the German/
      Latin original of Luther's works)

Introduction: Salvation as Union

1. Salvation in Christianity and Other Religions

All major religions agree on one thing: the deepest desire of the human person is to get in contact and to live in union with his or her God.[1] Different religions offer distinctive understandings about the nature of that union, and the way to the attainment of salvation. These differences notwithstanding, it seems reasonable to argue that salvation involves some form of union with God. Thus, the desire for union is the theme of religions and consequently theologies. Let us not be too naïve, however, I am not suggesting that all religions are equally valid ways of salvation; nor am I arguing that it does not matter what one believes and how one lives to be saved. I leave those thorny questions out of my considerations here to the lively debates in the theology of religions.

What I am saying here is simply that: any religion that wants to redeem its promises should give an answer to the most profound question of human life, namely, what is the way back to God, to live with God, to live in God and share in the divine? Christian theology from the beginning has offered an answer to the world and its followers in the form of the doctrine of deification and/or union with God. Even though the Eastern wing of the church has been the major carrier of this doctrine through the patristic era to our days, never has it been the sole treasure of one part of Christendom. The Western church has approached the idea of union with the help of different vocabulary.

[1] Cf. M. C. McDaniel, "Salvation as Justification and *Theosis*," in *A Lutheran-Orthodox Dialogue*, J. Meyendorff and R. Tobias, eds. (Minneapolis: Augsburg Fortress Press, 1992) 67.

The Orthodox Georgios I. Mantzaridis reminds us of the fact that the idea of deification, oneness with God, God-likeness, is "that which from the beginning has constituted the innermost longing of man's existence." Unfortunately, the first human person, in attempting to appropriate it by transgressing God's command, failed, and in place of deification met with corruption and death.

> Adam of old was deceived:
> Wanting to be God he failed to be God.
> God becomes man,
> So that He may make Adam god.[2]

This search for union with God is undoubtedly the leading motif in religions. For Hinduism, the religion that shapes the life of a significant segment of humanity currently, death is the unsurpassed question. Beneath their cosmic purposes, Vedic sacrifices were designed to ward off death temporarily and attain a full life span for humans. A more total conquest of death was the goal in the philosophies of the Upanishads, Buddhism, and Jainism. In Hinduism the idea of deification is connected with death. The cults of the deified dead add something new. Deification is looked upon as the means of death uniting the human being with God, rather than separating from the divine. Of course, given the cyclical nature of the Hindu worldview, the human-god continuum is a circle rather than deification being the endpoint.[3] It is clear that there are profound philosophical and religious differences between the idea of union in these Eastern religions and in the idea of deification in the Christian East. What I want to highlight here is the fact that the motif of union is so central an idea in all religions.

Recently it has been suggested that in the African context the traditional Eastern Orthodox idea of *theosis* may provide a challenging encounter with the African concept that has been called "vital participation": "We are convinced that the Bantu principle of vital participation can become the basis of a specifically African theological structure."[4] Commenting on this, Hartmunt Schönherr is ready to say that this "is the Orthodox concept contextualized for Africa."[5]

[2] "Doxastikon at the Praises," Feast of the Annunciation.
[3] For starters, see Stuart H. Blackburn, "Death and Deification: Folk Cults in Hinduism," *History of Religions* 24, no. 3 (1985) 255–74.
[4] V. Mulago, "Vital Participation," in *Biblical Revelation and African Beliefs*, Kwesi A. Dickson and Paul Ellingworth, eds. (Maryknoll, N.Y.: Orbis Books, 1969) 157.
[5] Hartmunt Schönherr, "Concepts of Salvation in Christianity," *Africa Theological Journal* 12, no. 3 (1983) 160.

But we need not go to the East or to Africa to find the same kind of spiritual yearning. Even in Europe and North America people look to crystals, signs, horoscopes, and generic angels for some sense of divine presence and purpose not unlike in eastern religions such as Buddhism. Could it be that the challenge of Christian theology is to speak of deification in a milieu that is permeated with the yearning for union of divine and human? M. M. Thomas of India, the former long-standing chairperson of the Central Committee of the World Council of Churches, has noted that "there is no question about the tremendous potentiality of a positive relation between orthodox spirituality and modernity."[6] The words of the Protestant F. W. Norris are both challenging and daring:

> Conforming to the world is not our goal. Yet by allowing our minds to be transformed, we may be prepared to contextualize the Gospel for this new wave of spirituality. To do that while still being true to Christian Tradition, we must recapture one great spiritual vision of Christian salvation which twentieth-century Protestants have largely ignored. *Koinonia*, fellowship with God, is actually deification, participation in God.[7]

Certainly, the early church and the fathers faced the same kind of challenges we do in today's postmodern cacophony of philosophical and religious voices. The use of *theosis* was daring. Non-Christians employed it to speak of pagan gods deifying creatures. The philosophers earlier on had used *theoo* in that way. It was not a Christian word first, nor was it only employed by Christians even after they made it central. But they cleaned it up and filled it up with a Christian meaning.[8]

The challenge of Christian theology lies not only in its encounter with other religions. It should also take account of modern philosophical and scientific culture. Some Christian philosophers have wondered whether the new open-ended view of reality in the sciences opens up new horizons for dialogue with Christian theology. For example, John Polkinghorne notes that in the midst of such discussions on the relationship between modern science and theology, the claim of Orthodox theologians may be correct, "that the true end of creation lies in deification."[9]

---

[6] M. M. Thomas' report delivered to the Central Committee in Berlin, August 1974, quoted in Hartmunt Schönherr, "Concepts of Salvation in Christianity," 162.

[7] F. W. Norris, "Deification: Consensual and Cogent," *Scottish Journal of Theology* 43, no. 4 (1996) 413.

[8] Norris, op. cit., 415.

[9] John Polkinghorne, *Reason and Reality: The Relationship between Science and Theology* (Philadelphia: Trinity Press International, 1991) 103.

Similarly, Arthur Peacocke, who in his book *Theology for a Scientific Age*, working to understand incarnation and salvation, opens part three with Irenaeus' famous comment about deification: God became human that we might become divine.[10] He also suggests that deification is probably "more congenial to an evolutionary perspective than the traditional, often Western, language of redemption, salvation, sanctification, etc."[11] Others have raised concerns about deification as a proper symbol for speaking of Christology and salvation vis-à-vis modern physics and philosophy,[12] but the discussion continues and new avenues are being opened up.

The thesis of this study is that amidst all the differences between the East and West with regard to theological orientations in general and the language and terminology of soteriology in particular, there is a common motif to be found: union with God. Both the Eastern understanding of *theosis* and the Western idea of justification have union as the ultimate goal. In the West, later Protestant soteriologies such as Anabaptism, Methodism, and most recently Pentecostalism have also expressed the idea of union, creatively combining Western and Eastern terminology and approaches. Finally, a corollary tentative proposal—even though the present study does not have a chance to pursue the question in any systematic way—suggests that the idea of union is also the dominant motif of all religions. Thus the idea of union with God has profound implications not only with regard to Christian ecumenism but also for a Christian theology of religions (the relationship of Christianity to other world religions).

2. Union in Salvation—Divisions in the Church

If it is the case that salvation is the dominant theme of religions, then soteriology, the doctrine of salvation, occupies a privileged place in theology. Carl E. Braaten has argued to this effect: "The whole of theology is inherently developed from a soteriological point of view, salvation is not one of the main topics, along with the doctrine of God,

---

[10] A. Peacocke, *Theology for a Scientific Age: Being and Becoming—Natural, Divine, and Human* (Minneapolis: Fortress Press, 1993) 189.

[11] Ibid., 430 n. 2; see also Norris, "Deification," 425–28.

[12] See M. J. Bozack, "Conjugate Properties and the Hypostatic Union," *Perspectives on Science and Christian Faith: Journal for the American Scientific Affiliation* 39 (1987) 105–7 who is skeptical of the use of deification mainly from the perspective of physics, and less from theology.

Christ, church, sacraments, eschatology and the like, it is rather the perspective from which all these subjects are interpreted."[13] Even though this statement betrays the specific interests of Lutheran theology, as a general principle it holds.

The challenge to Christian theology, though, is that the Christian church on earth is hopelessly divided in terms of doctrines, polities, tastes, leadership patterns, and so on. All Christians, however, want to give their distinctive testimony to one and the same God and God's Son, the Savior of all, Jesus Christ. According to the Christian understanding, all people, whether within or outside of the church, have the very same need: to be saved from fear and judgment to love and safety. Even though we believe and live our Christian lives within our various traditions, we do not suffer or die merely as Baptists, Catholics, Orthodox, or Pentecostals. Whether we like it or not, all Christians are on their way to the very same salvation provided by the same Almighty God. For Christian testimony to win any kind of credibility in an unbelieving and doubting world, we need a consensual understanding of salvation. Let us not be naïve: the Christian church is not likely to be united doctrinally, perhaps it even should not be. The richness of Christian theology and witness is the symphony—even though too often a cacophony—of various legitimate voices concerning the saving works of their God and Savior. While no homogenous testimony is to be expected or desired, a hope for a common perspective on salvation could be realistic.

The irony of Christianity lies in the fact that all Christians, as the rest of the world, yearn for union with God and unity between others. However, churches are divided, churches that speak about the final union to come. Could the doctrine of salvation be a catalyst for a more serious concern for unity?

Union with God, as God's greatest gift to the human being and the ultimate goal of human existence, has always been a prime consideration in the teachings on salvation of the church fathers, especially in the East.[14] True, Reformation theology has had a hard time in trying to reconcile the idea of *theosis* with the doctrine of justification. Historically, these two traditions have been considered diametrically opposed to each other.[15] A corollary problem is that—at least for Lutherans—the

[13] C. E. Braaten, *Principles of Lutheran Theology* (Philadelphia: Fortress Press, 1983) 63.
[14] Georgios I. Mantzaridis, *The Deification of Man: St. Gregory Palamas and the Orthodox Tradition*, Liadain Sherrard, trans. (Crestwood, N.Y.: St. Vladimir's Seminary Press, 1984) 12.
[15] See Georg Kretschmar, "Die Rezeption der orthodoxen Vergöttlichungslehre in der protestantischen Theologie," in *Luther und Theosis: Vergöttlichung als Thema der abendländischen*

Eastern soteriology entertains problematic notions of the freedom of the will, too positive an anthropology, and, worst of all, the idea of human-divine *synergia* in salvation. It is also a fact that poorly-read Protestants have insisted that the Eastern Orthodox "idolatrously make us all little gods or that they think of participation in the divine nature only in physical terms."[16] The great church historian Adolf von Harnack insisted that Irenaeus had adopted Gnostic ideas and misunderstood these concepts in physical ways.[17] Harnack is but an example of this kind of mindset.[18] It is almost amusing, if it were not so sad, that the United States Library of Congress cataloguing system puts the texts of Gregory Palamas, the leading Orthodox theologian, after the Gnostic texts of Nag Hammadi and before various Manichaean texts: the implication being that Palamas' theology of deification and Jesus-prayer belongs in the same category with Far Eastern mysticism and Manicheanism. These kinds of charges are both inaccurate and false.[19]

Ecumenically, it is highly interesting and also a learning experience to be reminded of the fact that whereas for Lutherans the doctrine of justification is the doctrine upon which Christianity either stands or falls, in the history of Orthodox theology there is almost a total absence of any mention of the idea of justification by faith. Whereas Calvin described justification by faith as the "hinge on which all true religion turned," the Eastern texts, for example the doctrinal manual of John of Damascus, *The Orthodox Faith*, never even mention the idea.[20] Or to take a more recent ecumenical case study, when the Roman Catholics and Lutherans have had bilateral talks since the close of the Vatican Council II, one of the main themes has been the doctrine of justification since it has had a church-dividing effect. In contrast, when the Roman Catholics and Pentecostals, currently the two biggest Christian families, representing well over one-half of all Christians, have carried on mutual dialogue—also from the beginning of the 1970s—the topic of justification has not even been mentioned in any of the final reports. The topic of salvation has been discussed intensively, but not from the

Theologie, Simo Peura and Antti Raunio, eds., Schriften der Luther-Agricola-Gesellschaft 25 (Helsinki and Erlangen: Martin-Luther Verlag, 1990) 61–80.

[16] Norris, op. cit., 418.

[17] Adolf Harnack, *History of Dogma,* Neil Buchanan, trans. (repr. New York: Dover Publications, 1961) 2:230–318.

[18] Further examples are provided by Georg Kretschmar, op. cit., 61–84.

[19] See further, Norris, op. cit., 418.

[20] See further, Daniel B. Clendenin, "Partakers of Divinity: The Orthodox Doctrine of Theosis," *Journal of Evangelical Theological Society* 37, no. 3 (1994) 366–69.

perspective of justification, but mainly from the perspective of the Spirit and related topics, such as the Spirit-baptism and its relation to water baptism, or conversion.

3. In Search of an Ecumenical Convergence

Caricatures concerning the nature of ecumenical theology abound. Some think it is mainly the same as what used to be called "controversial" theology, the purpose of which was to delineate confessional differences. Another less than accurate picture is to imagine that the sole purpose of ecumenism is to try to hide the differences and attempt a cheap consensus. Still another false view is that, with regard to main doctrines of Christianity, an agreement has to be reached as to what is the "right" formulation.

The ecumenical work on the doctrine of salvation is a good textbook example of the challenges and fruits of a real ecumenical theologizing. Three points deserve our attention here.[21] First, while admitting the difference of approaches to the question of salvation especially between the Eastern and Western churches—and these differences will become clear in the course of the present study, it does not necessarily mean that we should try to soften the differences. Perhaps it is the case that rather than trying to ease the tension, we should let the differing yet complementary Christian testimonies stand next to each other. The New Testament canon itself gives legitimacy to various conceptions of salvation. It is highly significant that none of the first seven ecumenical councils, binding for all Christian churches through the ages, defined the doctrine of salvation in any fixed way. There were other topics, such as the Trinity and Christology, which were defined in a much more exclusive way.

Second, the historical and even contemporary generalizations are not as neat and clean as some would have it. Although the West has been slow in characterizing the doctrine of salvation in terms of deification, it has never been unknown to the West. On the other hand, even though to the East the notion of justification and satisfaction are not so familiar, the problem of sin and the need for the sacrifice of the Lamb of God have always been acknowledged.[22]

Third, all Christian doctrines are responses to contextual and existential needs and challenges. Doctrines do not fall from heaven, nor are they constructions of theologians in need of extra work. Theology is

---

[21] Seed thought for my thinking here comes from Clendenin, op. cit., 368–69.

[22] Cf. E. Bentz, *The Eastern Orthodox Church: Its Thought and Life* (Garden City, N.Y.: Anchor Books, 1963) 43–47 especially.

but reflection on spirituality and felt needs in the church.[23] Hartmunt
Schönherr, writing specifically from an African perspective, divides the
symbols of salvation into three basic "archetypes," namely deification,
liberation, and justification. He notes that they exist in many variations
and that none of them is to be looked upon as the final candidate or the
exclusive one even though from an African perspective deification has
the potential of redeeming more promises. Concepts of salvation in Christianity are contextual and relative. He argues that in Africa a variety of
concepts of Christian salvation are needed, but not different salvations.[24]

The principle of contextualization has to be taken into account when
we look at Christian history. When all through the Medieval period in
the West there arose the need to highlight the juridical and legal aspects
of salvation, that was a contextual response to the feudal society. For us
living in the postmodern world, those images seem strange, since we
live in a totally different milieu. The Eastern church has always lived
next to great Eastern cultures and religions in which the question for
immortality and union with the divine has been the dominant question. The summary by Daniel B. Clendenin is balanced:

> In their better moments both western and Orthodox theologians acknowl-
> edge this point, that the Biblical material presents the work of Christ from
> a number of different perspectives and that all of them are necessary for
> a complete understanding of our salvation in Christ. Nevertheless a dif-
> ference of emphasis is still a genuine difference. The west lack any devel-
> oped notion of theosis and tends to express the idea of salvation in
> juridical categories. The eastern Church neglects the concept of justifica-
> tion in favor of deification, a theme that it discovers throughout the Bible
> and repeats down through the centuries.[25]

One of the most exciting things happening in ecumenical theology
currently is the fact that many Protestants are now rereading their heri-
tages through the church catholic. That includes reading them through
Eastern Orthodoxy. In this rereading the idea of union, even deification, is being reclaimed and reappropriated as one of the oldest, if not
the oldest Christian symbol of salvation.[26] Since the idea of union and

---

[23] See the important study by Paul Fiddes, *Past Event and Present Salvation: The Christian Idea of Atonement* (Louisville: Westminster/John Knox Press, 1988) who develops important criticism of many theories of salvation as systematic explanations. He wonders
whether they are actually more like extended analogies or illustration.

[24] Schönherr, "Concepts of Salvation in Christianity," 164–65.

[25] Clendenin, op. cit., 369.

[26] See also Norris, op. cit., 411.

deification is in fact an ancient Christian symbol of salvation, not totally foreign to mainline Protestantism either, "deification should be viewed by Protestants not as an oddity of Orthodox theology but as an ecumenical consensus, a catholic teaching of the Church, best preserved and developed by the Orthodox."[27]

Ecumenically, it is important to note that the idea of deification has never been so strange to the western Catholic Church. Recently, a Roman Catholic theologian has claimed—even if a bit of an overstatement—that "the Roman Catholic Church has always taught the deification of man through God's grace."[28] Hans Urs von Balthasar, the most creative theologian of the Roman church, has offered a contemporary reappropriation of the doctrine of deification in his own tradition.[29] The reason for a much more positive view among Roman Catholics probably has to do with their anthropology and a view of salvation which gives more weight to human responsibility; these two concepts have, in fact, been the main targets of the traditional Reformation critique of Catholic soteriology.

The plan of this book is the following. First, I will summarize the main contributions of current New Testament studies to the main theme of the book. Second, I will offer a historical survey of the doctrine of *theosis* in Eastern Theology, a selective and limited survey which only highlights topics and contributions relevant to the argumentation of the present work. Third, I will attempt to review the new pespective on Luther's theology as it has emerged largely at the University of Helsinki, the so-called "Mannermaa school." Fourth, I will survey the idea of union in other Protestant soteriologies including in Free Church theologies which rarely receive much attention. Fifth—the heart of the book—I will critically study contemporary ecumenical conversations concerning salvation, focusing on the issues of justification and deification and attempting to place them in a clear perspective. Finally, the last chapter pulls together the book's themes and outlines an ecumenical proposal for further study and reflection. Of course, the most that can be done in the present work is to highlight key perspectives and point to future tasks.

[27] Norris, op. cit., 422.
[28] Miguel Garijo-Guembe, "Schwesterkirchen im Dialog," *Catholica* (1994) 285. A Comparative Perspective," *Pro Ecclesia* 5 (1996) 203.
[29] Hans Urs von Balthasar, *Theologik*, vol. 3: *Der Geist der Wahrheit* (Basel: Johannes Verlag, 1987) 169ff.

2

Justification in Recent
New Testament Scholarship

The doctrine of justification, the chief article of faith of classical Reformation theology, the doctrine upon which the church either stands or falls, has come under serious scrutiny in recent years, especially in New Testament scholarship.[1] The leading figure in questioning the classical canons of the doctrine of justification by faith as it has been developed by Luther and his followers has been E. P. Sanders, whose work *Paul and Palestinian Judaism*[2] has placed Paul's relation to the Jewish religion of his time in a new light. The debate continues and not all are convinced about the proposal of Sanders and others, but there is no way to talk about justification and related terms without critical interaction with this new outlook in biblical studies. James D. G. Dunn, one of the participants in the most recent debates, has put the topic of justification in a proper perspective in light of New Testament scholarship:

> Luther's conversion experience and the insight which it gave him also began a tradition in Biblical interpretation, which has resulted for many in the loss or neglect of other crucial Biblical insights related to the same

[1] For a recent survey, see D. A. Carson, ed., *Right With God: Justification in the Bible and the World* (Grand Rapids, Mich.: Baker and Carlisle: Paternoster, 1992).

[2] E. P. Sanders, *Paul and Palestinian Judaism: A Comparison of Patterns of Religion* (Philadelphia: Fortress Press, 1977). Another formative work of his has been *Paul, the Law and the Jewish People* (Philadelphia: Fortress Press, 1983). An important study in this connection which has appeared after the writing of this book is Stephen Westerholm, *Perspectives Old and New on Paul: The "Lutheran" Paul and His Critics* (Grand Rapids, Mich.: Eerdmans, 2004).

theme of divine justice. And particularly in the case of Paul, Luther's discovery of "justification by faith" and the theological impetus it gave
especially to Lutheran theology has involved a significant misunderstand-
ing of Paul, not least in relation to "justification by faith" itself.[3]

By this comment, which summarizes much of the results of recent
New Testament study, Dunn is not saying that the doctrine of justification by faith is necessarily "wrong" as much as it is one-sided and perhaps misguided by some questionable assumptions. He acknowledges
the fact that the Protestant doctrine of justification has been a restate-
ment of central biblical insights related to salvation. So with his criticism he does not "mean to detract from or diminish this aspect which has
been so prominent in Reformation-inspired exegesis and teaching."
Still, it is important for Dunn that "other aspects be brought more fully
into the light so that in turn their value may once again be appreciated
and their influence felt to fuller effects."[4]

Now, what then are the issues contemporary New Testament research wants to challenge in the earlier approach to the topic of justification? Dunn summarizes them in the following way: First, Luther
understood Paul's conversion as the climax of a long, inward spiritual
struggle, something similar to that of Augustine who applied Romans 7
to his pre-Christian experience. Second, Luther thought of the doctrine
of justification in individualistic terms. Third, for Luther, Paul's discovery of justification by faith meant a turning away from Judaism. Fourth,
consequently, Luther regarded the Judaism of the New Testament times
as a degenerate religion, not unlike the Catholicism of Luther's own day.

With regard to the first point, it is clear that it has been often assumed that Luther understood Romans 7 as a reference to preconversion
time; Augustine certainly understood that passage so.[5] The problem is
that whenever Paul is talking about his preconversion experience, there
is no hint whatsoever of any agony of conscience (e.g., Gal 1:13-14).[6]
Dunn is also right with his reference to the individualistic understanding
of justification; not only did Luther understand salvation mainly with reference to individuals, but so has the mainstream of Western soteriology.

[3] J.D.G. Dunn, "The Justice of God: A Renewed Perspective on Justification by Faith,"
Journal of Theological Studies NS 43 (1992) 2.
[4] Ibid., 2.
[5] Cf. Gerald Bray, "Justification: The Reformers and Recent New Testament Scholarship," *Churchman* 109, no. 2 (1995) 103.
[6] This was already noted by the Lutheran Krister Stendahl, "The Apostle Paul and
the Introspective Conscience of the West," in *Paul among Jews and Gentiles* (Philadelphia:
Fortress Press/London: SCM Press, 1977) 78–96.

For Paul, however, especially in his main two letters in which he discusses the issue of justification, the focus is relational, namely relationship between the Jews as the elected people and the Gentiles, as the outsiders to the covenant.[7] And we always have to remind ourselves of the fact that Paul based his doctrine of justification on the Old Testament, the Jewish Bible. In Old Testament thinking *righteousness* is a relational concept. In fact, it has become clear that in Hebrew thought righteousness is a concept of *relation*; people are righteous when they meet the claims which others have on them by virtue of their relationships.[8]

Dunn wonders whether the influence of Bultmann's existentialism with its extreme focus on the individual has reinforced Luther's own individualism in the twentieth century.[9] There is no doubt about the validity of the third point, namely that Luther set Paul's new religion and Judaism in opposition to each other in a significant way. However, even with his well-known anti-Semitism, it is perhaps more legitimate to say that Luther never solved the problem of Christianity's relation to Judaism and he perhaps expressed various, even contradictory opinions on that. There is a strong opinion in recent New Testament scholarship that despite all his opposition to the *law* Paul experienced a conversion within Judaism and was always aware of his initial calling to preach Christ to the Jews.[10] Finally, the view of Judaism as a degenerate, legalistic religion is in need of serious reconsideration. Jewish scholars have reminded us for years that such a view of Palestinian Judaism in Jesus' time is not the Judaism they knew.[11] It has been the legacy of Sanders and other non-Jews to paint another picture of Judaism of that time as a religion of grace, with human obedience always understood as a response to that grace. "The covenant was given by divine initiative and the law provided the framework for life within the covenant, the means of living within the covenant, not a means of acceptance into the covenant in the first place."[12] As Dunn aptly notes, the "Judaism of what

[7] This is again supported by Stendahl, op. cit., 1–2.

[8] This was already noticed in the beginning of the twentieth century by H. Cremer, *Die paulinische Rechtfertigungslehre in Zusammenhange ihrer geschichtlichen Voraussetzungen* (Gütersloh: Bertelsmann, 1900); see further Dunn, op. cit., 16.

[9] Dunn, op. cit., 4; Bray, op. cit., 103–4 argues that Luther's theology of baptism would have led him to a less individualistic and more collective orientation, but I do not find his argument convincing.

[10] See, e.g., A. Segal, *Paul the Convert: The Apostolate and Apostasy of Saul the Pharisee* (New Haven: Yale University Press, 1990).

[11] For examples, see Sanders, *Paul and Palestinian Judaism*, 4–8.

[12] Dunn, op. cit., 8; see also p. 7.

Sanders christened as 'covenantal nomism' can now be seen to preach good Protestant doctrine: that grace is always prior; that human effort is ever the response to divine initiative; that good works are the fruit and not the root of salvation."[13]

On other questions regarding justification recent New Testament scholarship has reached a virtual consensus. Hardly anybody would support the claim that justification/righteousness is the center of Paul's theology. It can be a central idea to Paul,[14] but it is highly questionable whether justification or any other single theme would qualify as a center of Paul's thought.[15] Furthermore, contemporary scholarship in general agrees with the proposal of Ernst Käsemann[16] that justification and sanctification cannot be separated as they have been in Reformation theology, and even the Lutheran confessions (though not in Luther's own writings as will become evident in the course of the present investigation).

One of the most heated debates in biblical scholarship has centered on the precise meaning of the term "righteousness/justification" (*dikaiosyne*).[17] Dunn suggests that among the many justifiable translations, such as "justification," "righteousness," and "justice," the last one should be preferred. This is to correct the shift of Protestantism from the "justice of God" to "justification by faith."[18] For Bultmann, the meaning of the term "righteousness of God" denoted the gift of God that God has bestowed on those who have entered into the right relationship to him, and this being based on faith rather than on works.[19] Käsemann has made a proposal which while highly debated has become the starting point for future reflections. For him, the term "righteousness of

[13] Ibid., 8.

[14] M. A. Seifrid, *Justification by Faith: The Origin and Development of a Central Pauline Theme* (Leiden: Brill, 1992); see also P. T. O'Brien, "Justification in Paul and Some Crucial Issues of the Last Two Decades," in Carson, op. cit., 69–95.

[15] A good illustration of the shift in recent scholarship is the work by Ralph Martin, *Reconciliation: A Study of Paul's Theology* (Atlanta: John Knox Press, 1981) in which he argued for reconciliation as the theological center. In the recent reprint (Pasadena, Calif.: Wipf & Stock, 2000) he adopts the position that not even reconciliation would qualify as the center.

[16] E. Käsemann, "'The Righteousness of God' in Paul," in *New Testament Questions of Today*, W. J. Montague, trans. (Philadelphia: Fortress Press, 1969) 168–82.

[17] For a careful recent survey, see John Reumann, "Justification and Justice in the New Testament," *Horizons in Biblical Theology* 21, no. 1 (1999) 26–45.

[18] Dunn, op. cit., 21.

[19] R. Bultmann, *Theology of the New Testament*, K. Grobel, trans. (New York: Scribners, 1951) vol. 1: 271–72, 279–85.

God" was a Jewish apocalyptic concept that had to be distinguished from mere "righteousness" whether this was understood as a divine gift or as a human achievement. Käsemann does not understand the concept of "justification" as a forensic imputation; rather he sees it more in ontological terms. He also believes that in Jewish apocalyptic the "righteousness of God" was connected with an "obedience-producing power," the idea of which goes to the individual, referring to the hope of the salvation of the whole world.[20]

Recently, N. T. Wright has paid attention to the fact that in order to understand correctly the term "righteousness of God" its relationship to the covenant has to be established.[21] The major difference, though, is that in the Old Testament the covenant community was defined by external boundary markers, whereas in the New Testament it is governed by faith in Christ.[22] Wright summarizes his view:

> Paul is thus offering a doctrine of God, and of the people of God, which is built firmly on Christ and the Spirit, and in which the people of God are known, not by race or moral behaviour, but by Spirit-inspired faith in the God revealed in Jesus. Here is the doctrine of justification as it appears in Romans 9–11: Christian faith alone is the index of membership.[23]

In this way, the thorny question of the relationship between law and gospel, described by Luther as "the supreme art in Christianity,"[24] has been taken up by recent scholarship. According to A. von Harnack's famous interpretation from the beginning of the twentieth century, Paul never set these terms in antithesis.[25] Rather, Paul contrasted the law with faith (Rom 3:21ff.; 4:13ff.) or grace (Rom 6:14-15) or the Spirit (Rom 7:6).[26] Neither did Jesus completely do away with law, nor treat it, as the teaching of the Reformers often seems to imply, mainly negatively as a "mir-

---

[20] Bray, op. cit., 107–8; see further Käsemann, *Perspectives on Paul*, Margaret Kohl, trans. (Philadelphia: Fortress Press and London: SCM Press, 1971). For criticism, see, e.g., Seifrid, *Justification by Faith.*

[21] N. T. Wright, *The Climax of the Covenant* (Edinburgh: T. & T. Clark, 1991). Earlier on, Krister Stendahl, a major dialogue partner with Käsemann, criticized him for neglecting the role of "salvation history," which leads to the divorce of the concept of righteousness from the biblical context (*Paul among Jews and Gentiles* [Philadelphia: Fortress Press, 1976]).

[22] Wright, op. cit., 148–51.

[23] Ibid., 255.

[24] WA 36, 9, 28–29.

[25] A. von Harnack, *The Constitution and Law of the Church in the First Three Centuries* (London, 1910) 301–2.

[26] Wolfhart Pannenberg, *Systematic Theology*, Geoffrey Bromiley, trans. (Grand Rapids, Mich.: Eerdmans, 1998) vol. 3: 61.

ror" of our sinfulness to drive us to Christ. There is no doubt about the fact that Jesus' view of law differed from other Jewish views, but "less by its content, focused on love of God and neighbor, than on the basis that he offered for this content by not arguing from the authority of the legal tradition, although he too could remind his hearers of this tradition." Instead, Jesus based his statements on the future inbreaking of God's kingdom. Rather than focusing on the individual rulings of the law, he opened up the possibilities of discovering the universally valid content of the law of God.[27]

According to Pannenberg, "For Paul the Mosaic law reached an end in Christ (Rom 10:4). The word *telos* here can also be taken to mean that Christ is called the goal toward which the law was directed in the providence of God."[28] Still, Christ's coming also meant the coming of the end of the law.[29] Why did the law come to an end with the coming of Christ? Because in the death of Christ for sin (Rom 3:25), God demonstrated his covenant righteousness to which we may respond by faith rather than by works of the law (Rom 3:2); we are righteous before God only through faith, not by works of the law (Rom 3:28). "Those who reject faith in God's action in Christ cannot profit from any works of the law because they refuse obedience to the righteousness of God, not responding to it, then, by what they themselves do (Rom 10:3). Only in this situation does clinging to the righteousness of works by which the Jewish people remains faithful to God's covenant become a righteousness of one's own in contrast to God's covenant righteousness (Rom 10:3)."[30] This righteousness of faith, though, is not alien to Abraham or the Jewish faith (Rom 3:31; Gen 15:6).

Now Paul's criticism of the law does not lie so much in its inability to save those who follow it but in the Jewish insistence that salvation is brought about by virtue of membership in the elected covenant people. Paul insisted, as did Jesus, that it is only by virtue of a response of faith rather than the legal righteousness of faith that salvation comes.[31] For Paul any kind of nationalistic pride of Judaism was an anathema; here Paul was simply echoing what Old Testament prophets such as Amos

[27] Ibid., 59–60; quotation on 59.
[28] Ibid., 62.
[29] Sanders, *Paul, the Law, and the Jewish People,* 38ff.; Heikki Räisänen, *Paul and the Law* (Philadelphia: Fortress Press, 1983) 16ff.
[30] Quotation from Pannenberg, op. cit., 63, with reference to Sanders, *Paul, the Law, and the Jewish People,* 37ff., Räisänen, *Paul and the Law,* 169–77.
[31] Sanders, *Paul and the Law,* 68–69; *Paul and Palestinian Judaism,* 442–47; Pannenberg, op. cit., 64.

(9:7) as well as the New Testament preachers such as John the Baptist (Matt 3:9), and, of course, Jesus himself (Matt 8:10-12), taught. For Paul, justification means that God accepts persons apart from their racial origin whether Jews or Gentiles (Rom 9:6-8). Justification, the right relationship with God, is being offered to all people, even Gentiles.[32]

The main perspectives and their theological implications concerning the emerging consensus—even though with many variations and with continuing debate—in recent New Testament scholarship concerning justification can be summarized as follows: First, justification is one of the many legitimate images of salvation in the Bible; it cannot be made *the* hermeneutical key.

Second, in line with Old Testament usage, the term *dikaiosyne* primarily means the *justice* of God. Even when Paul uses the terminology of "imputation," he is not suggesting that the essence of the doctrine of justification is "legal imputation"; Paul uses this legal image as *one* of the ways to illustrate *one* side of his doctrine.

Third, justification and sanctification cannot be distinguished from each other in the way Reformation theology—in contrast to both Roman Catholic and Orthodox theologies—has done. Justification means primarily making just, setting a person in a right relationship with God and with others.

Fourth, the standard Christian interpretation of Jewish religion and law has to be reassessed in light of Jesus' and Paul's teaching. Even though the question of whether God intended the law to be a means of salvation in any sense has to be left open for further investigation, the emphasis of Jesus was on the inbreaking of the kingdom in his own person. For Paul, Christ meant the end and goal of the law in that the covenant requirement had been met in Christ's cross, and that opens a possibility for a response of faith. Apart from that, membership even in the Jewish covenant community does not bring about salvation.

Fifth, justification is a new status and relationship to God by faith in Christ through the Spirit. It means union between the human person and her Creator.

Sixth, even when justification requires individual response, it is not merely individualistic: it is integrally related to God's saving purposes for the covenant community and to the coming of the kingdom of God. Righteousness is thus also a relational concept, being right with God and other people.

[32] See further, Dunn, op. cit., 14–15.

3

Deification in the
Eastern Orthodox Tradition

1. "Partakers in Divine Nature": *Theosis* in the Bible

"I say, 'You are gods'" (Ps 82:6). This phrase from the Old Testament,
quoted by our Lord Himself (Jn 10:34), has deeply marked the spiritual
imagination of Orthodoxy. In the Orthodox understanding Christianity
signifies not merely an adherence to certain dogmas, not merely an exte-
rior imitation of Christ through moral effort, but direct union with the
living God, the total transformation of the human person by divine grace
and glory—what the Greek Fathers termed "deification" or "divinization" *(theosis, theopoiesis)*. In the words of St. Basil the Great, man is nothing less than a creature that has received the order to *become god.*[1]

These words of the Orthodox Bishop Kallistos of Diokleia focus
our attention on the most distinctive heritage of Eastern Orthodoxy, the
church which claims to represent the oldest Christian tradition. Along
the same lines, Christoforous Stavropoulous wonders whether we are
willing to hear the voice of God in the Bible, "God speaks to us human
beings clearly and directly and He says . . . 'You are gods, sons of the
most high—all of you' (Ps 82:6 and John 10:34)." He keeps on asking:
"Do we understand the meaning of this calling? . . . As human beings
we each have this one, unique calling, to achieve Theosis."[2]

[1] Bishop Kallistos of Diokleia, Foreword to Georgios I. Mantzaridis, *The Deification of
Man* (Crestwood, N.Y.: St. Vladimir's Seminary Press, 1984) 7 (emphasis his).
[2] C. Stavropoulous, *Partakers of Divine Nature* (Minneapolis: Light and Life, 1976) 17–18.

The Bible offers a sufficient number of passages about human participation in God for it to be taken as an important image of salvation. But perhaps it does not speak about it as much as Eastern Orthodox theologians and some others, too,[3] sometimes lead us to understand. The two cardinal texts are 2 Peter 1:4 and Psalm 82:6, which Jesus cites in John 10:34-36a:

> Through these he has given us his very great and precious promises, so that through them you may participate in the divine nature and escape the corruption in the world caused by evil desires. (2 Pet 1:4)

> "I said, 'You are "gods";
>   you are all sons of the Most High.'" (Ps 82:6)

> Jesus answered them, "Is it not written in your Law, 'I have said you are gods'?" If he called them 'gods,' to whom the word of God came—and the Scripture cannot be broken—what about the one whom the Father set apart as his very own and sent into the world? (John 10:34-36a)

The Petrine passage accentuates one of the leading motifs in the Orthodox understanding of salvation, namely release from the corruption and mortality caused by the evil desires of the world. As will become clear in the course of our study, Eastern theology does not focus so much on guilt as on mortality as the main problem of humanity. In addition, in the East, the concept of sin is viewed as something human beings do and choose for themselves rather than something "hereditary" as a result of the first human beings' sin in the distant past. Cyril of Alexandria comments on this passage from 2 Peter 1:4 to note that we are all called to participate in divinity, not just a few "saints." Although Christ alone is God by nature, all people are called to become God "by participation." In such participation we become likenesses of Christ and perfect images of God the Father.[4]

---

[3] Cf. Daniel B. Clendenin, "Partakers of Divinity: The Orthodox Doctrine of Theosis," *Journal of the Evangelical Theological Society* 37, no. 3 (1994) 365–79: "The Bible speaks extensively about theosis, according to the Orthodox theologians, and thus so must we." This article and that of F. W. Norris ("Deification: Consensual and Cogent," *Scottish Journal of Theology* 43, no. 4 [1996] 411–28) are good introductions to the topic. Their weakness is, however, that they seem totally unaware of the ecumenically most radical reorientation with regard to the doctrine of *theosis*, namely the growing Reformation/Lutheran appreciation of deification (Norris, though, makes a passing, unfortunately bibliographically inaccurate, mention of it on 421, n. 26).

[4] See V. Lossky, *The Vision of God* (Crestwood, N.Y.: St. Vladimir's Seminary Press, 1973) 98; Clendenin, "Partakers of Divinity," 372.

Orthodox theologians claim that the doctrine has a solid biblical basis that goes beyond the two explicit texts mentioned above.[5] They refer to other biblical passages, such as Exodus 34:30 where Moses' face shone, or Exodus 7:1 which reveals that Aaron became a god to Pharaoh. The transfiguration of Peter on Mt. Tabor (Matt 17:4) is also considered another classic text. Orthodox fathers often cite 2 Corinthians 8:9, Hebrews 4:15, and a host of texts from the Johannine corpus (John 3:8; 14:21-23; 15:4-8; 17:21-23; 1 John 3:2; 4:12).[6]

In a discussion of the idea of *theosis* in the Bible, based largely on Maximos the Confessor, Jaroslav Pelikan points out that the idea goes beyond a few individual passages of Scripture:

> The purpose of the Lord's Prayer was to point to the mystery of deifica-tion. Baptism was "in the name of the life-giving and deifying Trinity." When the guests at the wedding in Cana of Galilee . . . said that their host had "kept the good wine until now," they were referring to the Word of God, saved for the last, by which men were made divine. When, in the Epistles of the same apostle John, "the Theologian," it was said that "it does not yet appear what we shall be," this was a reference to "the future deification of those who have now been made children of God." When the apostle Paul spoke of "the riches" of the saints, this, too meant deification.[7]

Even when the objection is raised that often these texts are taken out of context Orthodox exegetes are not overly concerned. Even nowadays, Eastern theologians feel much more comfortable with the idea of spiritual interpretation.[8]

Orthodox theology is lived theology rather than analytical specu-lation. In fact, definite limits are set on human inquiry into things di-vine by *apophatic* theology, characteristic of Orthodoxy, that proceeds mainly by negation. What theology is able to say about God and God's dealings with humanity are mainly what these things are *not* rather than what they are.

The idea of *theosis* permeates much of the liturgy and prayer life in the Eastern church. A good example is the Canon for Matins of Holy Thursday in which the church confesses in its worship: "In my kingdom,

---

[5] E.g., Timothy Ware, *The Orthodox Church* (London: Penguin, 1964) 236–37.

[6] For a comprehensive listing of texts, see Clendenin, op. cit., 369ff.

[7] Jaroslav Pelikan, *The Spirit of Eastern Christianity* [The Christian Tradition, vol. 2] (Chicago: University of Chicago Press, 1974) 10.

[8] See John Breck, "Orthodox Principles of Biblical Interpretation," *St. Vladimir's Theo-logical Quarterly*, 40 (1996) 77.

said Christ, I shall be God with you as god."[9] The ancient liturgy of St. James proclaims:

> Thou has united, O Lord, Thy divinity with our humanity and our humanity with Thy divinity,
> Thy life with our mortality and our mortality with Thy life; Thou hast received what was ours and has given unto us what was Thine, for the life and salvation of our souls, praise be to Thee in eternity.[10]

2. The Renewal of the Image of God and Immortality

To gain a proper perspective on the Eastern view of salvation, we have to be aware of its distinctive anthropological outlook and its implications. In the main, Eastern anthropology looks forward to the renewing of the image of God. The underlying anthropology[11] is not necessarily more positive but, instead of operating mainly in guilt-concepts, it looks upward, so to speak, to the image of God to be fulfilled in mortal human beings.[12] This sets the tone for the rest of soteriology and theology in general.

The view of the human being in the Christian East is based upon the notion of "participation" in God. This "natural" participation, however, is not a static givenness; rather, it is a challenge, and the human being is called to grow in divine life. Divine life is a gift, but also a task which is to be accomplished by a free human effort.[13]

A person becomes the perfect image of God by discovering his or her likeness to God, which is the perfection of the nature common to all human beings. The Greek term *homoiousios*, which corresponds to *likeness* in Genesis 1:26, means precisely that dynamic progress and growth in divine life and implies human freedom. In Greek patristic thought there is no opposition between freedom (likeness) and grace (God's image in human beings): the presence in man of divine qualities, of a "grace" (God's image) which makes him fully man, "neither destroys his freedom, nor limits the necessity for him to become fully

---

[9] Quoted in Ware, *The Orthodox Church*, 236.

[10] Quoted in N. Arseniev, *Mysticism and the Eastern Church* (Crestwood, N.Y.: St. Vladimir's Seminary Press, 1979) 148. For this and the previous liturgical text, I am indebted to Clendenin, "Partakers in Divinity," 372.

[11] See the relevant sections in John Meyendorff, *Byzantine Theology: Historical Trends and Doctrinal Themes* (New York: Fordham University Press, 1974) ch. 11.

[12] See, e.g., Meyendorff, *Byzantine Theology*, 161ff.

[13] Ibid., 138–39 especially.

himself by his own effort: rather it secures that cooperation, or *synergy*, between the divine will and human choice which makes possible the progress 'from glory to glory' and the assimilation of man to the divine dignity for which he was created."[14]

Unlike much of classical Western theology, the Eastern fathers never viewed the creation of human beings as perfect even before the Fall. Humans were created imperfect and they had to be tested as free rational beings in order to become perfect through the stages of growth and maturity. According to Irenaeus, in Paradise "'they were both naked and were not ashamed,' having been created a short time previously; they had not understanding of the procreation of children, for it was necessary that they should first come to adult age, and then multiply from that time onward."[15] The first human beings then fell during the growth period while they were still immature.

In the fourth century, St. Gregory of Nyssa was asked a difficult question about children who die young. The ascetic who asked this question was wondering what could really be achieved by his spiritual labors, when he knew for sure that he was going to commit sins that would hinder his entrance into the kingdom. So it seemed like the child who died young was better off. Gregory's answer reveals the basic orientation of Eastern theology. The human condition in the next life is not primarily a matter of justice, reward, and punishment. God's aim is rather to fulfill the purpose for which he created human beings, namely, to participate in God's life. The earthly life is for growth and development for this eternal communion.[16] From this perspective it becomes understandable that according to Irenaeus, God originally intended that humans would enter into *theosis* through a natural process of growth. This process would have involved an education in love, a free collaboration with God.[17] Unfortunately, sin deflected humanity from this path and disrupted God's purposes.[18]

What then is the effect of the Fall in Eastern theology? Rather than thinking in terms of Augustinian transmittal of corrupted nature from

[14] Constantine N. Tsirpanlis, *Introduction to Eastern Patristic Thought and Orthodox Theology*, Theology and Life Series 30 (Collegeville: Liturgical Press, 1991) 46, quoting Meyendorff, op. cit., 139.

[15] Quoted in Tsirpanlis, op. cit., 47.

[16] Gregory of Nyssa, *De infantibus praemature abripiuntur* (*Patrologia Graece* 46: 17780 [J.-P. Migne]). I am indebted for this story to Nonna Verna Harrison, "Theosis as Salvation: An Orthodox Perspective," *Pro Ecclesia* 6, no. 4 (Fall 1997) 430–31.

[17] Irenaeus, *Adversus haereses* 4.38. 1–3.

[18] See further, Harrison, op. cit., 432–33.

generation to generation, Eastern thought focuses on two interrelated effects of the Fall: physical death and the obscuring or distortion of the image of God. Adam's sin was a personal choice and act, not a collective sin nor a "sin of nature." Hence, inherited guilt is impossible. The consensus of the Greek fathers, especially John Chrysostom, Cyril of Alexandria, Athanasius the Great, Gregory of Nyssa, and Maximos Confessor, emphasizes this critical point quite often.

According to Constantine N. Tsirpanlis, this view in the East differs from the Western counterpart in several crucial respects. In opposition to the Western anthropology, influenced by Augustine's sharp polemics against Pelagius, the Eastern view of human beings and the Fall is critical of the understanding of original sin and its influences: "1) as inherited guilt; 2) as total destruction of God's image in the human being; 3) as a 'sin of nature' and not a 'personal sin' of Adam and Eve; and 4) as legalistic relations of human beings with God and salvation based on Christ's death as satisfaction of divine justice."[19]

In the East, the cross of Christ is envisaged not so much as the punishment of the just one, which "satisfies" transcendent Justice requiring a retribution for human beings' sin. Rather, "the death of the Cross was effective, not as the death of an Innocent One, but as the death of the Incarnate Lord."[20] The point was not to satisfy a legal requirement, but to vanquish death. God alone is able to vanquish death, because he "alone has immortality" (1 Tim 6:16).[21] It is noteworthy that Eastern theology never produced any significant elaboration of the Pauline doctrine of justification. Even the commentaries on Romans and Galatians by the Fathers generally interpreted passages such as Galatians 3:13 as victory over death and sanctification of life. Understandably, the Eastern fathers also never developed the theory of "satisfaction" along the lines of Anselm's theory. As Meyendorff puts it, "The voluntary assumption of human mortality by the Logos was an act of God's condescension by which he united to himself the whole of Humanity." According to Meyendorff, this is what Gregory of Nazianzus taught when he said, "What is not assumed is not healed, and what is united to God is saved"; therefore, "we needed a God made flesh and put to death in order that we could live again.[22] One of the preferred images of the effects of Christ's

---

[19] Tsirpanlis, op. cit., 52.

[20] Georges Florovsky, "The Lamb of God," *Scottish Journal of Theology* (March 1961) 24.

[21] Meyendorff, op. cit., 16.

[22] Meyendorff, op. cit., 160, with quotations from Gregory of Nazianzus, *Ep.* 101 *ad Cledonium* and *Hom.* 45 respectively.

death in the Christian East has been "medical": the cross is an antidote to the poison of corruptibility and sin.[23]

A clear example of the orientation of Eastern anthropology and Christology is offered by a quote from Athanasius in which he reflects on the meaning of the cross in light of the mortality of human beings:

> Thus, taking a body like our own, because all our bodies were liable to the corruption of death, He surrendered His body to death in place of all, and offered it to the Father. This He did out of sheer love for us, so that in His death all might die, and the law of death thereby be abolished because when He had fulfilled in His body that for which it was appointed, it was thereafter voided of its power for men. This He did that He might turn again to incorruption men who had turned back to corruption, and make them alive through death by the appropriation of His body and by the grace of His resurrection. Thus He would make death to disappear from them as utterly as straw from fire.[24]

Eastern anthropology accepts punishment, death, and mortality, not as God's retribution or revenge for sin as much as pedagogy. The human being's finitude would make repentance well up within her, the possibility of free love to God, the Creator and the source of all life. And, "God's plan has not changed; He always desires that man should be united with Him and transfigure the whole earth. The whole history of humanity will thus be that of salvation."[25] As microcosm the human being represents and assimilates in herself the whole macrocosm, the creation. What happens to human beings, happens to creation. God is the Savior of all.

The above-mentioned two major results of the Fall, namely physical death and the distortion of the image of God, call for the regaining of immortality and the restoration of the image. Salvation, then, is not primarily viewed as liberation from sin even though that is not a matter of indifference, but rather as a return to life immortal and the reshaping of the human being into the image of her creator. These two elements constitute the two greatest reasons for the incarnation of the Son of God. Consequently, Eastern theology takes the New Testament term *soteria* (salvation) in its biblical sense, which goes beyond terms

[23] E.g., John of Damascus, *De imaginibus* 3, 9.

[24] Athanasius, *De Incarnatione Verbi Dei*, "On the Incarnation," trans. and ed., A Religious of C.S.M.V., Intr. C. S. Lewis (Crestwood, N.Y.: St. Vladimir's Seminary Press, 1996) 34 [hereafter CSMV]. For the doctrine of incarnation and its relationship to deification in Athanasius, see Constantine N. Tsirpanlis, *Greek Patristic Theology: Basic Doctrines in Eastern Church Fathers*, Monograph Series in Orthodox Theology and Civilization 3 (New York: EO Press, 1979) 25–39.

[25] Tsirpanlis, op. cit., 53.

such as "redemption," "reconciliation," "justification," and the like to encompass the wholeness of new life under God.

God did not "fail" in the creation of human beings. If, like Athanasius and others argued, God is the embodiment of truthfulness and goodness, then incarnation means the restoration of human beings and the creation:

> It was unworthy of the goodness of God that creatures made by Him should be brought to nothing through the deceit wrought upon man by the devil; and it was supremely unfitting that the work of God in mankind should disappear, either through their own negligence or through the deceit of evil spirits . . . [S]uch indifference to the ruin of His own work before His very eyes would argue not goodness in God but limitation. . . . Yet, true though this is, it is not the whole matter. . . . [I]t was unthinkable that God, the Father of Truth, should go back upon His word regarding death in order to ensure our continued existence. He could not falsify Himself. . . .[26]

The perfect God-man was the only qualified person to sum up in his own life the corruptibility and distortion of the image and bring about a "recapitulation" of the whole human race and creation.

> We have seen that to change the corruptible to incorruption was proper to none other than the Saviour Himself, Who in the beginning made all things out of nothing; that only the Image of the Father could re-create the likeness of the Image in men, that none save our Lord Jesus Christ could give to mortals immortality, and that only the Word Who orders all things and is alone the Father's true and sole-begotten Son could teach men about Him and abolish the worship of idols. . . . In the same act also He showed Himself mightier than death, displaying His own body incorruptible as the first-fruits of the resurrection.[27]

3. The Eastern Fathers, Incarnation, and the Deifying Spirit

Orthodox theology is based on the teaching and witness of the church fathers. Even though theologizing in the Eastern wing of the Christian church is currently as vivid as it has ever been, its task is not to construct new doctrines but creatively, in light of what the Spirit is teaching, to reinterpret and help reappropriate the ancient teachings of the fathers. The doctrine of deification is a grand example of this living tradition; the basic orientation of Eastern theology was fashioned during the postbiblical and patristic period.

---

[26] Athanasius, *De Inc.*, 6, 7 [CSMV, 32–43].
[27] Ibid., 20 [CSMV, 48–49].

The Orthodox John Zizioulas has argued that one of the reasons for the separation of the Eastern and Western traditions since the early patristic period is their epistemological difference. Generally speaking, the Eastern church, borrowing primarily from Greek philosophy, has been principally concerned with those realities that are beyond history, while the West, borrowing more from the Jewish tradition, is more conscious of the positive aspect of revelation, of all that it adds to the knowledge that man can acquire by natural reason.[28] These epistemological differences bear upon the doctrines of anthropology and soteriology.

Even though Orthodox Vladimir Lossky's comment that theosis is "echoed by the fathers and the theologians of every age"[29] might intentionally be an overstatement, it does reflect the general mindset of the fathers. Their understanding of salvation was shaped by the idea of participating in the very essence of God. The patristic doctrine of *theosis* can be briefly formulated as follows:

> Divine life has manifested itself in Christ. In the church as the body of Christ, man has a share in this life. Man partakes thereby of "the divine nature" (2 Pet 1:4). This "nature," or divine life, permeates the being of man like a leaven in order to restore it to its original condition as *imago Dei*.[30]

Another term used for deification/divinization is "Christification." This is based on the idea that there is a christological structure to the human being and the destiny of humanity is to be found in Christ.[31] *Theosis* is the mystery of human nature's perfection in Christ, not its alteration or destruction, because *theosis* is the mystery of eternal life in communion with God in the divine Logos.[32]

The theological background to the prominence of the idea of deification in Eastern soteriology is the emphasis of the Eastern fathers on

---

[28] J. Zizioulas, *Being as Communion* (Crestwood, N.Y.: St. Vladimir's Seminary Press and London: Darton, Longman & Todd, 1985) 68 and "Preserving God's Creation," *King's Theological Review* 12 (1989) 2. See also Paul Negrut, "Orthodox Soteriology: *Theosis*," *Churchman* 109, no. 2 (1995) 154–70 for a detailed treatment of the influences of these epistemological differences on the doctrine of salvation in the East.

[29] V. Lossky, *The Mystical Theology of the Eastern Church* (Crestwood, N.Y.: St. Vladimir's Seminary Press, 1976) 134. See also Georgios Mantzaridis, op. cit., 105.

[30] Tuomo Mannermaa, "Theosis as a Subject of Finnish Luther Research," *Pro Ecclesia* 4, no. 1 (1995) 42.

[31] See, e.g., Pananyiotis Nellas, *Deification in Christ: The Nature of the Human Person*, tr. Norman Russell (Crestwood, N.Y.: St. Vladimir's Seminary Press, 1987) 23–42, 121–40.

[32] Kenneth Paul Wesche, "Eastern Orthodox Spirituality: Union with God in *Theosis*," *Theology Today* 56, no. 1 (1999) 31.

the incarnation and the role of the Spirit[33] who communicates the grace that deifies humans and makes them sharers of divine life. They believed that through the incarnation the mortal had been changed into immortal and the passible into impassible. The great Eastern teachers, Athanasius, both Gregorys, and Cyril of Alexandria, insisted that it was by the incarnation of the Logos that humanity was anointed by the Holy Spirit. According to Cyril, "Christ filled his whole body with the life-giving power of the Spirit. . . . It was not the flesh that gave life to the Spirit, but the power of the Spirit that gave life to the flesh."[34]

With regard to *theosis,* the two patristic[35] texts most often cited are from Irenaeus and Athanasius. Irenaeus: "The word of God, our Lord Jesus Christ . . . did through His transcendent Love, become what we are, that He might bring us to be even what He is Himself."[36] Athanasius: "He, indeed, assumed humanity that we might become God."[37] Still another early text from Origen is a favored one: according to him, when we transcend the material realm the contemplation of God is brought to "its proper fulfillment," which fulfillment is the spirit "to be deified by that which it contemplates."[38] Many other examples from the Eastern fathers could be added, for example, from Gregory of Nyssa who said, "God united Himself to our nature in order that our nature might be made divine through union with God."[39] Another Gregory, of Nazianzus, echoes this by saying that as God became incarnate, man became divinized, and that to the extent that Christ became a real man, so we become real gods.[40]

For Athanasius, the emphasis on deification comes also from his opposition to the Arian heresy, which was also a theory of deification,

---

[33] For the main sources see Congar, *I Believe in the Holy Spirit* (New York: Herder, 1997) esp. vol. 1, 73–77 and vol. 3, 29–35. For a more detailed exposition, see C. N. Tsirpanlis, op. cit., and Stanley M. Burgess, *The Holy Spirit: Eastern Christian Traditions* (Peabody, Mass.: Hendrickson, 1989).

[34] Quoted in Congar, op. cit., vol. 1, 73.

[35] For a detailed treatment of some selected patristic texts/authors, see Panayiotis Nellas, op. cit., and Donald Winslow, *The Dynamics of Salvation: A Study in Gregory of Nazianzus,* Patristic Monograph Series 7 (Cambridge, Mass.: Philadelphia Patristic Foundation, 1979). A sample of representative texts, relevant to the purposes of the present theme, is also to be found in Stanley M. Burgess, *The Holy Spirit: Eastern Christian Traditions* (Peabody, Mass.: Hendrickson, 1989).

[36] Irenaeus, *Ad. Haer.* 5.

[37] Athanasius, *De Incarnatione,* 54 [CSMV, 93].

[38] Quoted in Lossky, *Vision of God,* 61–62 [PG 14:817].

[39] Gregory of Nyssa, *Oratio Catechetica* 25; cf. Clendenin, "Partakes," 371.

[40] Gregory Nazianzus, *Epistle* 101; *Logos* 29.29; *Poemata dogmatica* 10.5-9.; see also Basil, *On the Holy Spirit* 1.2; cf. Clendenin, "Partakers," 371, n. 34, 35.

although in the judgment of the mainstream Christian theology a false one. Arianism considered Christ the first creature who was deified in a very special way, though still like us. Athanasius responded to that by saying that what in itself proves the full divinity of the Word is that we are deified through and in him.[41]

Many more patristic texts could be added from the Cappadocian fathers and others. Basil attributes the experience of *theosis* to the Holy Spirit who, "being God by nature . . . deifies by grace those who still belong to a nature subject to change."[42] St. Macarius likewise accentuates the role of the Spirit in *theosis* when he says that persons to be deified, though they retain their own identity (i.e., do not overstep the distinction between God and humans), "are all filled with the Holy Spirit."[43]

Maximos the Confessor describes deification as a participation of the "whole man" in the "whole God":

> In the same way in which the soul and the body are united, God should become accessible for participation by the soul, through the soul's intermediary, by the body, in order that the soul might receive an unchanging character, and the body, immortality; and finally that the whole man should become God, deified by the grace of God-become-man, becoming whole man, soul and body, by nature, and becoming whole God, soul and body, by grace.[44]

Maximos continues by saying that a person "who becomes obedient to God in all things hears God saying: 'I said: you are gods' [Jn 10:34]; he then is God and is called 'God' not by nature or by relation but by [divine] decree and grace."[45] It is not, however, through her own activity or "energy" that a human being can be deified—this would be Pelagianism—but by divine "energy"; the two energies have a synergy that has an ontological basis in Christ.[46]

4. The Palamite Vision of Salvation

The greatest individual theologian of the Christian East, Gregory Palamas (1296–1359), monk of Mount Athos and archbishop of

[41] Cf. Tsirpanlis, op. cit., 66.

[42] Basil, *On the Holy Spirit* 1.2, quoted in Lossky, *The Vision of God*, 80 [PG 29:665].

[43] Cited in Clendenin, "Partakers," 374; cf. Kallistos Ware, *The Orthodox Way* (Crestwood, N.Y.: St. Vladimir's Seminary Press, 1990) 168.

[44] Maximos the Confessor, Book of *Ambiguities,* quoted in Meyendorff, *Byzantine Theology,* 164 [PG 91:1088].

[45] Ibid., quoted in Meyendorff, op. cit., 164 [PG 91:1237].

[46] Cf. Meyendorff, op. cit., 164–65.

Thessalonike, never presented a systematic doctrine of divinization, but his contribution to the topic has been enormous. Regardless of the controversial debates with his theological opponents and the resulting reactionary nature of his theology, Gregory is highly esteemed as the teacher of divinity and a man of prayer.[47]

Building on the teachings and spirituality of the fathers, Palamas built his teaching on deification on these three premises: (1) the creation of the human being "in the image and after the likeness of God"; (2) the incarnation of the Logos of God; and (3) the strength of the human being's communion with God in the Holy Spirit.[48]

Palamas often reminds us of the fact that even though human beings were created in God's image, they are the image in a sort of indistinct way, whereas Christ is an identical image. Human beings, having their origin in God, in their existence mirror God and owe their life totally to the Creator. As such, true life springs from their participation in the life of God and communion with him. Now it is the task of the incarnation of the Son to help us grow into the full realization of that image. In a sermon delivered on Holy Saturday, Palamas expounds the motif of the divine incarnation by saying that "God's Son became man to show to what heights He would raise us; to keep us from self-exaltation through thinking that we ourselves have secured the revocation of our fall; to join together, as a true mediator, and as Himself being both divine and human, the sundered aspects of our nature . . . to purify the defilement that sin introduced into our flesh."[49]

This was made possible by virtue of the hypostatic union in Christ's person of the divine and human.[50] When the Logos of God took on human nature, he bestowed on it the fullness of his grace and delivered it from the bonds of corruption and death. The consequence of this hypostatic union of the two natures in Christ was the deification of the human nature. This view of Palamas is sometimes called in the East the "physical" view, since it derives the deification of human nature from its hypostatic union with the incarnate Logos of God.

> In the person of Christ existed, in its entirety, human nature individually particularized, which, being hypostatically unified with the Logos of God, was deified and received the fullness of the divine energy. For Palamas

---

[47] One of the most well-known aspects of Palamas's life has to do with the Jesus prayer and the Hesychastic controversies around it. See further, Metropolitan Nicolae Corneanu, "The Jesus Prayer and Deification," *St. Vladimir's Theological Quarterly* 39, no. 1 (1995) 3–24.

[48] See further Mantzaridis, *The Deification of Man*, 15–39.

[49] Gregory Palamas, *Homily*, 16, quoted in Mantzaridis, 25–27.

[50] See further, Mantzaridis, op. cit., 28.

and the Orthodox tradition, the flesh of Christ, being the body of the Logos of God incarnate, is the point of man's contact with God.[51]

One of the most delightful pictures Palamas uses is this: through the deification of Christ's human nature, the "first-fruits of our substance" were deified, and a "new root" was created, capable of instilling life and incorruptibility into its shoots.[52]

It should be clear by now that for Palamas as well as Athanasius and the other fathers, any diminution of the divine or human nature of Christ is not just a question of theology, it relates to anthropology as well. If Christ himself were a creature, then he could not have brought about union with God; on the contrary, Christ would have been in need of union himself. Palamas strongly opposed Christologies with those tendencies.[53]

Even though Palamas's view of salvation builds on the incarnation, it is also pneumatologically loaded. Taking notice of the biblical passage that teaches that the love of God flows into the hearts of the faithful through the Holy Spirit (Rom 5:5), he writes: "Not through rational thought, but through the Holy Spirit within us do we achieve the experience of love and the gifts it bestows."[54] Christ could not have entered the church after his ascension had not the Spirit already deified Christ's human nature in the incarnation of the Logos.

The grace of the Holy Spirit penetrates the soul of the human being because it is uncreated. According to Palamas, no created thing may unite with the human soul. Those of the faithful who participate in the uncreated grace of the Spirit achieve a lasting regenerative quality and are rendered "spiritual." For Palamas, as for the fathers, the sacraments are the created media which transmit the uncreated grace of God. The human being as a created being has need of these created means if she is to approach and receive the uncreated grace of the Holy Spirit. Baptism is the initiatory access to the grace and the eucharist the sustaining power.[55]

5. *Theosis* as the Defining Principle of the Doctrine of Salvation in Eastern Theology

As has become evident, there is a pronounced difference in orientation in Christology and soteriology between the East and West. According

---

[51] Ibid., 30.
[52] Gregory Palamas, *Defense of the Hesychasts* 3.1.33, quoted in Mantzaridis, 30.
[53] Mantzaridis, op. cit., 32–33.
[54] Gregory Palamas, *Defense of the Hesychasts* 2.1.28, quoted in Mantzaridis, 34.
[55] See further, Mantzaridis, op. cit., 41–60.

to Eastern theology, Latin traditions have been dominated by legal, juridical, and forensic categories. Eastern theology, on the contrary, understands the need of salvation in terms of deliverance from mortality and corruption for life everlasting. Union with God is the goal of the Christian life, even becoming "in-godded."[56] The idea of divine-human cooperation in salvation is not only accepted but is enthusiastically championed, although it is not understood as nullifying the role of grace.

According to the Eastern view, "the descent *(katábasis)* of the divine person of Christ makes human persons capable of an ascent *(anábasis)* in the Holy Spirit. It was necessary that the voluntary humiliation, the redemptive *kénosis*, of the Son of God should take place, so that fallen men and women might accomplish their vocation of *theosis*, the deification of created beings by uncreated grace."[57]

Eastern theologians do not speak of deification only as a metaphor; they also stress the reality of the union with God, promised to the faithful. According to V. Lossky, "The words of St. Peter are explicit: *partakers of the divine nature*. They leave us in no doubt as to the reality of the union with God which is promised us, and set before us as our final end, the blessedness of the age to come. It would be childish, not to say impious, to see in these words only a rhetorical expression or metaphor."[58] Orthodox theology, of course, struggles with the compatibility of the two seemingly opposite ideas: the absolute incommunicability of the divine being and a real partaking of humanity in God. They argue that the distinction between God and the human person is not nullified. God still remains God and humans remain human though participating in the divine. Orthodox theology has tried to solve this problem by making a distinction between divine essence and divine energies. According to the Eastern understanding, deification means participating in divine energies, not the divine essence as such. The classical formulation is that of Gregory Palamas.[59] Whatever one may think of this

---

[56] For succinct expositions of the basic ideas of the doctrine of *theosis* in Eastern theology, see Vladimir Lossky, *In the Image and Likeness of God* (Crestwood, N.Y.: St. Vladimir's Seminary Press, 1985), ch. 5 entitled, "Redemption and Deification," especially 97–98; Lossky, *Mystical Theology*, ch. 10 entitled, "The Way of Union"; Meyendorff, op. cit., 159–65 especially.

[57] Lossky, "Redemption and Deification," in *In the Image and Likeness of God,* 97–98.

[58] Lossky, *Mystical Theology,* 67.

[59] Hannu T. Kamppuri, "Theosis in der Theologie des Gregorios Palamas," in *Luther und Theosis: Vergöttlichung als Thema der abendländischen Theologie,* ed. Simo Peura and Antti Raunio, Schriften der Luther-Agricola-Gesellschaft 25 (Helsinki and Erlangen: Martin-Luther Verlag, 1990) 49–60.

model, there is no denying the passion of Eastern theology to affirm the idea of the divine-human union. It is also clear that for Orthodox theology deification has nothing to do with pantheism; the essence of human nature is not lost and can never be identified with the general concept of divinity.

In this sense we have to say that human *theosis*, even though real, is a relative rather than an absolute transformation. "There is a real and genuine union of the believer with God, but it is not a literal fusion or confusion in which the integrity of human nature is compromised." Orthodoxy consistently rejects the idea that humans participate in the essence or nature of God. So, at no point, even when deified, is our humanity diminished or destroyed.[60] Maximos the Confessor states it accurately: "All that God is, except for an identity in *ousia* [essence], one becomes when one is deified by grace."[61]

Various facets of the meaning of deification are highlighted by the rich vocabulary of Eastern theology with regard to salvation. Terms such as transformation, union, participation, partaking, intermingling, elevation, interpenetration, transmutation, commingling, assimilation, reintegration, adoption, recreation are used to refer to the same reality.[62]

The deification of the creature will be, of course, realized in its fullness only in the age to come. This deifying union nevertheless has to be fulfilled ever more and more even in this present life. Consequently, Eastern theologians do not shy away from speaking of divine-human *synergy*,[63] the cooperation of the person with God. Men and women are saved by grace, but not without one's total devotion and willingness to be transformed.

Prayer, asceticism, meditation, humble service, and similar exercises are recommended for the attainment of this noble goal. The notion of merit, though, is foreign to the Eastern tradition. In general, their attitude towards grace and free will is less reserved than their Western partners. In the East, the question of free will has never had the urgency that it assumed in the West from the time of St. Augustine onward. The Eastern tradition never separates grace and human freedom. Therefore,

[60] Clendenin, "Partakers of Divinity," 373.
[61] Maximos the Confessor, *Book of Ambiguities*, 41, quoted in Clendenin, "Partakers," 375.
[62] Ware, *The Orthodox Way*, 168.
[63] The idea of *synergy* relates to other theological *loci* in Eastern theology; e.g., the doctrine of the inspiration of Scripture is understood as a cooperative effort between the Spirit and the human instrument who receives divine revelation. See John Breck, "Orthodox Principles of Biblical Interpretation," *St. Vladimir's Theological Quarterly* 40, nos. 1 & 2 (1996) 77ff.

the charge of Pelagianism (i.e., that grace is a reward for the merit of the human will) is not fair. It is not a question of merit(s), but of cooperation, of a synergy of the two wills, divine and human. "Grace is a presence of God within us which demands constant effort on our part . . ."[64] In the nineteenth century, Bishop Theophanes, a great Russian ascetic writer, asserted that "the Holy Ghost, acting within us, accomplishes with us our salvation" and that "being assisted by grace, man accomplished the work of his salvation."[65]

6. Spirit and *Theosis:*
The Pneumatological Soteriology of the East

John Meyendorff speaks to one of the most distinctive characteristics of Eastern theology in saying that the "early Christian understanding of creation and of man's ultimate destiny is inseparable from pneumatology."[66] It has always been the task of the Eastern wing of the church to keep alive the pneumatological orientation. Even though Vladimir Lossky's criticism of Western theology for its lack of pneumatological orientation sounds like an overstatement—he argues that by the time of Anselm of Canterbury the West had already lost the true idea of the person of the Holy Spirit, "relegating Him to a secondary position by making Him into a kind of lieutenant or deputy of the Son"— it is well worth hearing. Lossky is probably right in that too often Western soteriologies have been Christocentric and neglected a proper pneumatological focus. A healthy soteriology needs a balance between the work of Christ and the Spirit.[67]

Since the divine Spirit is the Giver of life, his main soteriological operation is the divinization of human beings.[68] So the role of the Holy Spirit in Eastern soteriology is highlighted by the ultimate goal of salvation. Redemption has our salvation from sin as an immediate aim, but salvation will have its ultimate realization in the age to come in our union with God, the deification of the created beings whom Christ ransomed. But this final realization involves the dispensation of the Holy

[64] Lossky, *Mystical Theology*, 198; see also 196–97.

[65] Cited in Lossky, *Mystical Theology*, 199.

[66] Meyendorff, op. cit., 13.

[67] Lossky, "Redemption and Deification" in *In the Image and Likeness of God*, 103, see also 97–110.

[68] Burgess, *The Holy Spirit: Eastern Christian Traditions*, 1–9. See also Don Fairbairn, "Salvation as *Theosis:* The Teaching of Eastern Orthodoxy," *Themelios* 23, no. 3 (1998) 42–43.

Spirit. The work of the Spirit is, of course, inseparable from that of the Son. In the words of St. Athanasius, "God bearing flesh," and Christians, "bearing the Spirit."[69]

As we have noticed, in Eastern thought salvation is understood essentially in terms of participation and communion with the deified humanity in the incarnate Logos. The Eastern fathers even dare to call the Spirit the "image of the Son"; by this they imply the truth that the Spirit is the main agent which makes communion a reality. According to Athanasius, the Son has given us "the first fruits of the Spirit, so that we may be transformed into sons of God, according to the image of the Son of God."[70] Thus, if it is through the Spirit that the Logos became a human being, it is also only through the Spirit that true life reaches us. As Nicholas Cabasilas summarized, "What is the effect and the result of the sufferings and works and teaching of Christ? Considered in relation to ourselves, it is nothing other than the descent of the Holy Spirit upon the Church."[71]

Lossky reminds us of the fact that the role of the Spirit in salvation is to confirm the personal dignity of the deified human person:

> If our individual natures are incorporated into the glorious humanity of Christ and enter the unity of His Body by baptism, conforming themselves to the death and resurrection of Christ, our persons need to be confirmed in their personal dignity by the Holy Spirit, so that each may freely realize his own union with the Divinity. Baptism—the sacrament of unity in Christ—needs to be complemented by chrismation—the sacrament of diversity in the Holy Spirit.[72]

Interestingly, the Eastern fathers attribute to the Spirit all the multiplicity of names that can be attributed to grace,[73] as is evident, for example, in St. Gregory Nazianzen and St. Basil. They freely speak about the Holy Spirit as effecting deification, perfection, adoption, and sanctification.[74] Eastern Christians sing, "The Holy Spirit giveth life to souls; he exalteth them in purity; He causeth the sole nature of the Trinity to

---

[69] Athanasius, *De incarnatione*, 8, quoted in Lossky, *The Vision of God*, 70 [PG 26:991]; cf. Lossky, "Redemption and Deification," 103ff.

[70] Athanasius, *De incarnatione*, 8, quoted in Meyendorff, *Byzantine Theology*, 171 [PG 26:997].

[71] Nicholas Cabasilas, *A Commentary on the Divine Liturgy*, 37, 3.

[72] Lossky, "Redemption and Deification," 108.

[73] For a careful analysis of the relation between grace and the Holy Spirit in Latin theology, see Wolfhart Pannenberg, *Systematic Theology*, G. W. Bromiley, trans. (Grand Rapids, Mich.: Eerdmans, 1998) vol. 3, 197–200.

[74] For representative texts, see Lossky, *Mystical Theology*, 163ff.

shine in them mysteriously."[75] The Eastern church teaches that that which is common to the Father and the Son is the divinity which the Holy Spirit communicates (cf. *perichoresis*) to humans within the church, in making them partakers of the divine nature.[76] According to Gregory Nazianzen, deification is the highest gift and blessing of the Holy Spirit.[77] In this sense, as St. Seraphim of Sarov said, "the true aim of the Christian life is the acquisition of the Holy Spirit of God."[78]

The Holy Spirit, however, always respects human freedom. The Spirit does not actually bring about the human being's deliverance but gives her access to the regenerative and divine work of Christ that has been accomplished once for all. And as Gregory Palamas often reminds us, it is only by means of the Holy Spirit that Christ himself enters the church and remains her head for all eternity. In the spirited church, the Holy Spirit is the contact point between the corrupted human being and the glorified God-bearing Logos.[79]

In fact, the idea of deification cannot be expressed on a Christological basis alone, but demands a pneumatological development as well. "For the mystical tradition of Eastern Christendom, Pentecost, which confers the presence of the Holy Spirit and the first-fruits of sanctification, signifies both the end and final goal . . . of the spiritual life."[80] It is important to note that in the Eastern rite of confirmation[81]—"anointing" with the Spirit—follows immediately upon baptism. The Holy Spirit is operative in both sacraments. The Spirit recreates human nature by "purifying it and uniting it" with the body of Christ. The Spirit also "bestows deity" upon human persons.[82] Eastern theology even speaks about Christians as "christs," anointed ones: The Spirit who rests like a royal unction upon the humanity of the Son communicates himself to each member of Christ's body.[83]

The mystical theology of the Eastern wing of the church is often more experience-based and concrete than Latin theology. Basil writes, "just as he who has grasped one end of a chain also draws along with

[75] Antiphon in the 4th tone from the Sunday Office.
[76] Lossky, *Mystical Theology*, 162. See also Wolfhart Pannenberg, *Systematic Theology*, vol. 1 (Grand Rapids, Mich.: Eerdmans, 1991) 266ff.
[77] See Tsirpanlis, *Introduction to Eastern Patristic Thought*, 168ff.
[78] Cited in Ware, *The Orthodox Church*, 230; see also Lossky, *Mystical Theology*, 196.
[79] See further, Mantzaridis, op. cit., 15.
[80] See Lossky, *Mystical Theology*, 170.
[81] For a fine exposition of confirmation-chrism in the Eastern tradition, see Tsirpanlis, *Introduction to Eastern Patristic Thought*, 111–15.
[82] See Lossky, *Mystical Theology*, 170.
[83] Ibid., 174.

him the other end, so he who draws the Spirit . . . through Him draws along both the Son and the Father."[84] The role of the Spirit in this understanding—although the language is of course not to be taken at face value—is to make the "first contact," to be followed by the revelation of the Son and, through him, the Father.[85] There is a genuine trinitarian outlook in the Eastern view: "The Father does all things by the Word in the Holy Spirit."[86]

There is an ancient rule according to which theology develops and is based on spirituality (*lex orandi lex credendi*, literally: the "law" [principle] of prayer becomes the "law" of believing [in the sense of the content of faith]). The way the doctrine of the Spirit emerged in the East confirms this rule. The focus on deification in the doctrine of salvation helped the Eastern fathers finally reach the understanding of the full deity of the Spirit. As is well known, it took considerable time for the Christian church to decide for the full deity of the Spirit as the deity of Christ was the primary focus in the beginning. It was the task of the Cappadocians to help convince the church that the Spirit belonged, both in equality and in dignity, to the holy Trinity. For Athanasius, the trinitarian baptismal formula showed that the Spirit shares the same divinity as the Father and the Son. Why? Because our deification requires it: if the Spirit is not consubstantial with the Father and the Son, the Spirit cannot make us conform to the Son and therefore cannot save us. For Athanasius and Basil, the Spirit has a relationship with the Son similar to that which the Son has with the Father.[87]

Basil's brother, Gregory of Nyssa (c. 330–c. 395), further developed the doctrine of the divinity of the Spirit on the basis of his doctrine of salvation. Building on his brother's and Athanasius' formulations, he argued that the formation (*morphosis*) of the Christian and his perfection (*teleiosis*) according to Christ's model are the work of the sanctifying Spirit; the Spirit therefore is consubstantial with the Son and the Father. In other words, there is a unity of *nature* but a distinction between *hypostases*.[88]

---

[84] St. Basil, *Letter* 38, Sr. Agnes Clare Way, trans. (New York: Fathers of the Church, 1951) 89–90 [PG 26:605].

[85] See Meyendorff, *Byzantine Theology*, 168 especially. For pneumatological implications in general, see ch. 13, "The Holy Spirit."

[86] Athanasius, *Ad Serap.* 1, 28, quoted in Meyendorff, *Byzantine Theology*, 171 [PG 26:596].

[87] Congar, op. cit., vol. 3:30.

[88] Congar, op. cit., vol. 3, 31–32.

There is a healthy theological balance in the Eastern doctrine of salvation between Christology and pneumatology. In the words of John Meyendorff:

> Examples can be easily multiplied, which show that the Byzantine theological tradition is constantly aware that in the "economy" of creation and salvation the Son and the Spirit are accomplished in one single divine act—without, however, being subordinated to one another in their hypostatic or personal existence. The "head" of the new, redeemed humanity is, of course, Christ, but the Spirit is not only Christ's agent; He is, in the words of John of Damascus . . . "Spirit of God, direct, ruling; the fountain of wisdom, life and holiness; God existing and addressed along with the Father and Son; uncreated, full, creative, all-ruling, all-effecting, all-powerful, of infinite power, Lord of all creation and not subject to any; deifying, not deified; filling, not filled; shared in, not sharing in; sanctifying, not sanctified."[89]

Having highlighted key Eastern ideas of salvation, in the next chapter we will take up perspectives on justification and deification offered by the "new interpretation" of Luther as pursued at the University of Helsinki, Finland. This new paradigm carries enormous ecumenical potential in relation both to Eastern Orthodox and Roman Catholic theology.

---

[89] Meyendorff, op. cit., 172, quoting John of Damascus, *De fide orth.* I, 8.

4

Justification and Deification in Martin Luther's Theology

1. A New Paradigm of Luther Interpretation

Research on Luther and his theology has been dominated and mentored by the German theological tradition. In Europe, since the 1970s a "new quest for Luther's theology" has emerged mainly at the University of Helsinki, initiated by Tuomo Mannermaa and his students. The Mannermaa School has provided a most promising and also to some extent controversial proposal about a new reading of Luther's own writings. Among other things, Mannermaa has claimed that *Luther's* view of justification differs in a significant way from the official *Lutheran* doctrine as expounded in the confessional books of the Evangelical Lutheran Churches.[1] The confessional documents were mainly drafted by Melanchthon, and rather than being an attempt to offer a constructive theology, they are an occasional response to Catholicism—even more so than Luther's own theology. The Mannermaa School rejects the distinction between justification and sanctification as foreign to Luther's thought. They claim that for Luther the doctrine of justification is not a forensic term but rather a matter of Christ abiding in the heart of the believer in a "real-ontic" way (a detailed explanation of this

[1] "Lutheran" has two meanings: it can denote either Martin Luther's theology as it is expressed in his own writings or the theology/theologies of Lutheran confessions and subsequent Lutheran formulations. During the discussion I will show that these two have to be distinguished from each other.

most controversial concept is given later in this study). They also believe that *theosis*, rather than being a foreign Orthodox concept, is in fact one of the images Luther used to describe salvation.

These findings have been rapidly introduced into ecumenical conversations, first between the Russian Orthodox Church and the Finnish Lutheran Church, and then into the international Orthodox-Lutheran dialogues. While still debated on both sides of the Atlantic Ocean, this new paradigm of Luther interpretation offers to the ecumenical world a most creative and challenging proposal. What makes it so appealing is its explicitly ecumenical orientation with regard to the Orthodox view on the one hand and the Roman Catholic on the other hand. Furthermore, in the extensive research of the Mannermaa School, an unprecedented pneumatological potential of Luther's theology has been recovered. An important impetus to the recovery of a pneumatological outlook in the doctrine of salvation came from the dialogue with the Orthodox Churches.[2]

The dissemination of the results and methodological orientations of this rapidly growing Scandinavian school of Luther studies has been very meager in the English-speaking academy on both sides of the Atlantic since the studies are written either in German, Finnish, or other Scandinavian languages. Not until 1998 was the first English monograph offered to the English speaking world: a collection of essays by Finnish Luther scholars, entitled *Union with Christ* (1988), edited by two American Lutheran theologians, Carl E. Braaten and Robert W. Jenson.

The main contribution of the Mannermaa School has been the creation of a new methodological framework for the interpretation of Luther.[3] As such, the main methodological thesis of the Mannermaa School is to

---

[2] A recent brief introduction in English to the methodological orientations and the main results of the Mannermaa School can be found in Tuomo Mannermaa, "Why is Luther so Fascinating? Modern Finnish Luther Research," in *Union with Christ: The New Finnish Interpretation of Luther*, Carl E. Braaten and Robert W. Jenson, eds. (Grand Rapids, Mich.: Eerdmans, 1998) 1–20.

[3] The main topics of research thus far have been the doctrine of justification in Luther and its relation to the Eastern Orthodox doctrine of *theosis* (see further, T. Mannermaa, *Der im Glauben gegenwärtige Christus: Rechtfertigung und Vergottung Zum ökumenischen Dialog*, Arbeiten zur Geschichte und Theologie des Luthertums, Neue Folge, Band 8 [Hannover, 1989], based on several writings in Finnish, the most important of which is *In ipsa fide Christus adest: Luterilaisen ja ortodoksisen kristinuskonkäsityksen leikkauspiste*, MESJ 30 [Vammala, 1979]); *theosis* in Luther's theology (see further, Simo Peura, *Mehr als ein Mensch? Die Vergöttlichung als Thema der Theologie Martin Luthers von 1513–1519*, Veröffentlichungen des Institut für Europäische Geschichte Mainz, Band 152 [Stuttgart, 1994]); the meaning of the "Golden Rule" in Luther (see further, Antti Raunio, *Die Summe des christlichen Lebens:*

criticize the neo-Protestant, neo-Kantian distinction between God's "essence" and "effects," which means that we do not have any means of knowing anything about God; we only can know the effects of God in our lives. This so-called "transcendental effect" orientation, originated by the German philosopher Hermann Lotze in the nineteenth century, has blurred the meaning of the real presence of Christ in Luther research, they claim.[4] This older paradigm has argued that Luther was moving beyond the old scholastic metaphysics with its idea of "essence" toward a more relational view of knowledge. Based on neo-Kantian philosophy, this view believes that theology cannot know anything about the "essence" (ontology) of God, only recognize his "effects" in us.[5] The Mannermaa School argues that this kind of reasoning does not reflect Luther's "realistic" ontology but rather is a later philosophical construction.[6]

Our discussion of Luther's theology of justification will proceed in the following way. First, we will take a look at the leading theological motif in Luther, namely, his theology of love—both divine and human love. This is integrally connected with his famous idea of the theology of the cross. These themes form the anthropological and theological background for his doctrine of justification by faith. Second, we will focus on the dominant motif in Luther's exposition of justification by faith, namely, Christ's presence in the believer and the consequent change it brings about. Third, we will be ready to inquire into the controversial claim of the Mannermaa School according to which one of the ways Luther understands justification is as *theosis*. Fourth, we will look at the implications of Luther's theology of justification and deification for neighbor love, and finally its pneumatological implications.

Die 'Goldene Regel' als Gesetz der Liebe in der Theologie Martin Luthers von 1510 bis 1527, Systemaattisen teologian laitoksen julkaisuja 13 [Universität Helsinki, 1993]; the book will be published in Germany by Veröffentlichungen des Instituts für Europäische Geschichte, Mainz). There are several projects underway, such as Luther's pneumatology and the doctrine of the Trinity.

[4] A full-scale study is offered by Risto Saarinen, *Gottes Wirken auf uns: Die transzendentale Deutung des Gegenwart-Christi-Motivs in der Lutherforschung* (Stuttgart: Franz Steiner, 1989).

[5] Also, in that older interpretation, it has been held that Luther's ontological orientation would be anti-metaphysical, emphasizing God's work *for me* without making any ontological commitments, in opposition to the Catholic view which embraces "metaphysical" categories, "substances" and "accidents." For an English synopsis, see Risto Saarinen, "The Presence of God in Luther's Theology," *Lutheran Quarterly* 3, no. 1 (1994) 3ff.

[6] See, e.g., Mannermaa, "Why Is Luther So Fascinating?" 4–9.

2. The Theology of Love and the Theology of the Cross

The new interpretation of Luther serves as a helpful critic and challenger of some earlier opinions that have almost gained the status of canons. One of these standard opinions has been that for Luther the theological breakthrough came as a result of his existential anguish as a monk trying to please an angry God. Supposedly, Luther finally discovered a gracious God who in his mercy declared the desperate seeker righteous. Apart from the existential circumstances in Luther's own life, it might be more fitting to think that Luther faced the very same kind of problem all Christians throughout history have encountered, namely, the question of love. Perhaps Luther was trying to work out a solid answer to the great commandment of Scripture: "You shall love the Lord your God with all your heart, and with all your soul, and with all your strength, and with all your mind; and your neighbor as yourself" (Luke 10:27). If so, it is not the doctrine of justification that is the key to Luther's theology, even though it is a central theme, but rather his theology of love. Indeed, Luther is first and foremost a theologian of love.[7] His view of God's love together with his famous distinction between two kinds of love, namely, "God's love" and "human love," functions as the organizing principle of his theology. Luther's understanding of love, though, is governed and shaped by his christological focus and especially the all-important role of the cross. Thus, to gain insight into the ethos of Luther's thinking about God and human beings, we need to begin by inquiring into his theology of love and related theology of the cross.

Luther presents the outline of his theology, in the form of a theology of love and of the cross, in his early Heidelberg Disputation (1518).[8] The leading idea in the Heidelberg Disputation, and in Luther's theology in general, is the difference between two kinds of love: *amor Dei* and *amor hominis*. The Disputation culminates in the last thesis: "The love of God does not find, but creates, that which is pleasing to it. . . . Rather than

---

[7] This is the basic thesis of Tuomo Mannermaa, *Kaksi rakkautta: Johdatus Lutherin uskonmaailmaan*, Suomalaisen Teologisen Kirjallisuusseuran julkaisuja 194, 2. painos (Helsinki: STKJ, 1995 [orig., 1983]); Mannermaa, "Why Is Luther So Fascinating?" 3: "Luther's entire theology takes on the character of a consistent theology of love." So also Simo Peura, "What God Gives Man Receives: Luther on Salvation," in *Union with Christ*, 76.

[8] A recent, full-scale study on the theology of cross as one of the leading motifs of Luther's theology is offered by Kari Kopperi, *Paradoksien Teologia: Lutherin disputaatio Heidelbergissä 1518* [Theology of Paradoxes: Luther's Heidelberg Disputation 1518] Teologisen Kirjallisuuden Julkaisuja 208 (Helsinki: STKJ, 1997).

seeking its own good, the love of God flows forth and bestows good."[9] Human love is oriented towards something inherently good in which self-love defines the content and the object of the love.[10] Men and women love something that they believe they can enjoy. Medieval scholastic theology provided an example for Luther of this kind of love.

God's love is the opposite of human love: it is directed towards something that does not exist in order to create something new. Luther sometimes calls God's love *amor crucis*: "This is the love of the cross, born of the cross, which turns in the direction where it does not find good which it may enjoy, but where it may confer good upon the bad and needy person."[11] It is born out of the cross of Christ and is manifested through God's gracious works in the world. In divine love the movement is downward, whereas in human love it is upward.[12] By this, Luther does not, however, deny the value of genuine human love per se;[13] his mode of speaking is *paradoxical*.

Luther goes a step further by arguing that the works born out of human love are in fact sin leading to death. Although good works seem to be good in other peoples' eyes, Luther calls them "deadly sins."[14] Luther's extremely negative attitude toward human works with regard to salvation is sometimes interpreted as nullifying all moral efforts. This is not what Luther means, for Luther sees a definite difference between "theological" and "moral" perspectives on works; it is the theological perspective in view here. In God's sight *(coram Deo)*, human works are not just worthless but dangerous as they blind the eyes of moral men and women to believe that their works have merit in relation to salvation. From this perspective it becomes understandable why Luther can bluntly say that something that human beings regard as a good work morally could be a deadly sin leading to damnation. Of course, Luther admits, human beings are capable of choosing rightly according to practical reason, in affairs pertaining to human life *(coram hominibis)*,

---

[9] *HDT* 28; *LW* 31, 57. Whenever the reference is to the *Heidelberg Disputation*, I also give its reference (number of the thesis). The most reliable original (Latin) version of the *Heidelberg Disputation* is found in Martin Luther, *Studienausgabe*, ed. Hans-Ulrich Delius et al. (Berlin: Evangelische Verlangsanstalt, 1979).

[10] Mannermaa, *Kaksi rakkautta*, 9–11.

[11] *HDT*, 28; *LW* 31, 57.

[12] Mannermaa, *Kaksi rakkautta*, 12–13. See *WA* 7, 547, 1–10 *(Magnificat)*.

[13] For example, sexual love between man and woman is highly appreciated by Luther. Mannermaa, *Kaksi rakkautta*, 14–15. A fine study of Luther's view of sexuality is Heiko O. Oberman, *Luther: Man between God and the Devil*, Eileen Walliser-Schwarzbart, trans. (New Haven and London: Yale University Press, 1989) especially 272–76.

[14] *HDT* 3, 5; *LW* 31, 43, 45. Kopperi, *Paradoksien teologia*, 103–14.

and he has no objection to the notion of free will in this regard, but even then what they seek is basically their own good. But in relation to things pertaining to God, the notion of free will is "an empty word" without any content.[15]

Rather than rewarding human works according to their (alleged) merits, God instead reveals their weakness and sinfulness through the cross and suffering.[16] Whereas good human works appear to be beautiful in man's eyes, God's works in this world often appear to be ugly. And whereas men do their best to become good and beautiful by seeking the good and beautiful, according to Luther, God works in the opposite way: God conceals Godself in lowliness to reveal the greatness of God's love.

The natural mind imagines the works of God to be beautiful, fine, and attractive, but according to Luther, the opposite is the case. God's works "are always unattractive and appear evil, (but) they are nevertheless really eternal merits," insofar as they are in accordance with his true love.[17] He describes the works of God with biblical imagery, citing Isaiah 53:2, "He had no form or comeliness,"[18] "The Lord kills and brings to life; he brings down to Sheol and raises up."[19] In other words, God makes us "nothing" *(nihil)* and "stupid" to reveal his real love to us.[20]

Here Luther introduces one major aspect of his "theology of paradoxes": God's alien work *(opus alienum Dei)* and God's proper work *(opus proprium Dei)*. God's alien work means putting down, killing, taking away hope, leading to desperation, and so on. God's proper work means the opposite: forgiving, giving mercy, taking up, saving, encouraging, and so on.[21] The following quote clearly depicts how Luther uses these two terms:

> You [God] exalt us when you humble us. You make us righteous when you make us sinners. You lead us to heaven when you cast us into hell. You grant us the victory when you cause us to be defended. You give us life when you permit us to be killed.[22]

[15] See, e.g., Luther's exposition on Romans in *WA* 56, 355–56.
[16] Kopperi, *Paradoksien teologia,* 115.
[17] *HDT* 17; *LW* 31, 44. Kopperi, *Paradoksien Teologia,* 115–18 especially. As a fitting conclusion to the section dealing with human works, Luther states that the only way to prepare for the receiving of grace is to preach about sin and the need for repentance (*HDT* 3; *LW* 31, 43).
[18] Isa 53:2.
[19] 2 Sam 2:6 (Luther mistakenly refers to 1 Kgs 2:6).
[20] *HDT* 4, *LW* 31, 43.
[21] *LW* 14, 95, etc.; Mannermaa, *Kaksi rakkautta,* 43.
[22] *LW* 14, 95.

The alien works Luther sometimes calls "the works of the left hand" and the proper works "the works of the right hand." It is important to understand that, while these two kinds of works seem to be the opposite of each other, they result from the same love of God. Luther in fact says that God's proper work is veiled in his alien work and takes place simultaneously with it.[23]

In acting thus God turns out to be the devil. To show the paradoxical nature of his theology of love and of the cross, Luther even goes so far as to say that God's works are not just veiled in their opposite but they also sometimes create bad results.[24] To illustrate his point, Luther compares the working of God in this world with a worker with a bad axe: although the worker himself is skillful, because of the tool the results are bad. Furthermore, Luther argues that sometimes God uses even Satan for his *opus alienum* in order to work out his *opus proprium*.[25]

The God who acts like this is a hidden God. In theses 19–24 of the Heidelberg Disputation, Luther turns to this aspect of his theology of the cross. The theologian of the cross observes God in the shame and lowliness of the cross, whereas the theologian of glory looks for God in majesty and glory.[26] In order to reveal Godself, God works through a process that could be described like this: (1) A human being is not able to reach God with the help of wisdom or works, since God is hidden; (2) The true wisdom and knowledge can be found only in the cross; (3) God makes a human being a *nihil*, (4) to make him/her a new being.[27]

With reference to Exodus 33:18–34:9 (especially 33:23), in which Moses asks God to show God's face, God responds: "But . . . you cannot see my face; for man shall not see me and live" (33:20 RSV). Instead, God lets Moses see God's back. On the basis of this event, Luther differentiates between God's visible properties such as humanity, weakness, and stupidity, and God's invisible properties such as virtue, divinity, wisdom, justice, and goodness.[28] The theologian of glory goes astray in that she attempts to know God "through the creatures," in other words by seeking God in the created order. In doing so, as Luther succinctly states, the theology of glory "calls evil good and good evil," whereas, "A theology of the cross calls the thing what it actually is."[29]

---

[23] *HDT* 16; *LW* 31, 50.
[24] *HDT* 5, 6; *LW* 31, 45.
[25] *HDT* 20; *LW* 31, 45.
[26] *HDT* 20; *LW* 31, 52.
[27] Kopperi, *Paradoksien teologia*, 128–29.
[28] *HDT* 20; *LW* 31, 52.
[29] *HDT* 21; *LW* 31, 53.

The integral connection between the theology of the cross and a theology of love comes to focus in Luther's view of new birth: "To be born anew, one must consequently first die and then be raised up with the Son of Man. To die, I say, means to feel death at hand."[30] In order to save a human being, God first kills her by God's alien work; this is the work of "annihilation," only then God begins God's proper work and causes new birth.[31]

In fact, the idea of "annihilation," or "nothing" *(nihil)* is one of the crucial concepts in Luther and is organically related to both his theology of love and of the cross as well as to his insistence on justification as the presence of Christ in the believer.[32] Luther joins the classical and medieval theological metaphysics in maintaining that our being is being as participation in God. This applies to both our being in the "natural state" and in the state of grace, although there is a difference of degree between these two, especially in view of the fact that in the *esse gratiae* there is participation in God through Christ.

It is against this background that the frequency of Luther's use of *nihil* comes to light. It has two main connotations: on the one hand, it denotes total dependence—ontological dependence—of the human being on God. The human being is *nihil ex se*, she has no existence of her own but is totally dependent on God both for existence and activity. On the other hand, *nihil* in Luther is also an indication of the sinfulness of the human being. For Luther, sin can be identified in the formal sense with *nihil*.

This dual "being as *nihil*" of a human being is an objective fact for Luther; however, a natural man or woman does not acknowledge this state before God. A human being is not willing to acknowledge the state of *nihil* but rather attempts to be just in both natural and spiritual essence. The tragedy of this alleged "being something" is that God is not allowed to be God. For Luther, God according to God's very nature is *creator ex nihilo* who in God's *agape*-love wants to give good gifts and create new things. Therefore, to let God be who God is, the Creator and Sustainer, a human being has to be made what he/she really is, i.e., *nihil*. For this alien work, Luther uses terms such as "making [the human being] as

---

[30] *HDT* 24; *LW* 31, 55.

[31] *HDT* 16; *LW* 31, 50, 51.

[32] The basic study here is Sammeli Juntunen, *Der Begriff des Nichts bei Luther in den Jahren von 1510 bis 1523*. Schriften der Luther-Agricola-Gesellschaft, Bd. 36 (Helsinki: Luther-Agricola Society, 1996). For a synopsis in English, see Juntunen, "Luther and Metaphysics: What is the Structure of Being according to Luther?" in *Union with Christ*, 129–60.

nothing." Its purpose, though, is not the destruction of a human being but total transformation.

In the final analysis, even annihilation is to be understood as a result of God's love. Its goal is the emergence of a new being, and the destruction of false human love. It also results in the real knowledge of self, not based on the human being's own capacity but on God. But—and this Juntunen emphasizes against the older interpretation tradition—this "making into nothing" means for Luther more than just a transformation of knowledge *(cognitio)*, in other words, that the person simply acknowledges her state or even undergoes an emotional change *(affectus)* in which the human being no longer loves herself as an independent entity. Rather, it means a "real" transformation of the human.[33]

This paradoxical work of God, however, is nothing foreign to God. According to Luther this kind of "action which is alien to God's nature results in a deed belonging to his very nature."[34] The purpose of this paradoxical work is to free a human being from a false presumption in order for her to open up to God's love which, as we have seen, is directed towards the sinful, weak, and nothing to make it holy, strong, and wise.[35] Putting their trust in human love, men and women in fact rely on the creature and thus do not allow God to be God. The root of evil and the bedrock of all sin for Luther is pride and perverted self-confidence.

> He, however, who has emptied himself through suffering no longer does works but knows that God works and does all things in him. For this reason, whether God does works or not, it is all the same to him.[36]

In the final analysis, it is not love but rather faith that makes our relationship to God possible, namely the faith that is not something that men and women choose for themselves but is a gift from God. Faith changes human will in such a way that through their works they are not seeking good for themselves but for others as well.

3. Justification as the Presence of Christ and Deification

For the Mannermaa School, the leading idea in Luther's theology of salvation and justification is Luther's insistence on "Christ present in faith" *(in ipsa fide Christus adest)*. In other words, Christ in both his person

---

[33] Juntunen, *Der Begriff des Nichts bei Luther,* 411.
[34] *HDT* 16; *LW* 31, 51.
[35] *HDT* 16; *LW* 31, 50–51.
[36] *HDT* 24; *LW* 31, 55.

and his work is present in faith and is through this presence identical with the righteousness of faith. The Lutheran tradition holds to the idea of God living in the believer *(inhabitatio Dei)*. This for Mannermaa is analogous with the doctrine of *theosis*. According to Luther, Christ and thus his person and work is present in faith itself.[37] Or to put it in another way, the Christ present in faith is the *forma fidei*, the realization or concrete manifestation of faith. Mannermaa summarizes: "Thus, the notion that Christ is present in the Christian occupies a much more central place in the theology of Luther than in the Lutheranism subsequent to him. The idea of a divine life in Christ who is really present in faith lies at the very center of the theology of the Reformer."[38]

This view, traditionally called "justification," can also be called *theosis* according to the ancient doctrine of the fathers with whom Luther agreed. Justification and deification, then, mean the "participation" of the believer in Christ which, because Christ is God, is also a participation in God himself. This participation is the result of God's love: human beings cannot participate in God on the basis of their own love; rather God's love effects their deification. Christian participation in Christ thus is the result of the divine presence in the believer as love. This participation, following Athanasius and others, is a participation in the very *ousia* of God. There is, then, what the Mannermaa School calls a "real-ontic"[39] unity between Christ and the Christian, though the substances themselves do not change into something else. What makes the claim of this new paradigm unique—and controversial especially with regard to the established canons of German Luther interpretation—is that the idea of Christ's presence is "real-ontic," not just a subjective experience or God's "effect" on the believer as the neo-Protestant school has exclusively held.

[37] Mannermaa, "Theosis," 42–44.

[38] Mannermaa, "Why is Luther So Fascinating?" 2. For a synopsis in English, see Mannermaa, "Theosis as a Subject of Finnish Luther Research," *Pro Ecclesia* 4, no. 1 (1995) 37–48 and Mannermaa, "Justification and *Theosis* in Lutheran-Orthodox Perspective," in *Union with Christ*, 25–41. See also Eeva Martikainen, "Die Unio im Brennpunkt der theologischen Forschung," in *Unio: Gott und Mensch in der nachreformatorischen Theologie*, E. Martikainen, ed. (Helsinki: Luther-Agricola-Gesellschaft, 1996) 13–18.

[39] For a critical philosophical scrutiny and critique of this concept in Lutheran studies, see Dennis Bielfeldt, "The Ontology of Deification," in *Caritas Dei: Beiträge zum Verständnis Luthers und der gegenwärtigen Ökumene*, Festschrift für Tuomo Mannermaa zum 60. Geburtstag, Oswald Bayer, Robert W. Jenson, and Simo Knuuttila, eds. (Helsinki: Luther-Agricola-Gesellschaft, 1997) 90–113; see also Bielfeldt, "Response" [to "Luther and Metaphysics: What is the Structure of Being According to Luther?" by Sammeli Juntunen] in *Union with Christ*, 161–66. Bielfeldt offers and critically scrutinizes several complementary models to describe the "presence" of Christ in the believer in Luther's theology.

Ecumenically, it is extremely fruitful that as a result of this new interpretation of Luther an unprecedented convergence between the traditional Orthodox view of salvation as *theosis* and Luther's doctrine of justification as Christ's presence in the believer could be found. Even though Luther does not often use the concept of *theosis*,[40] his theology clearly leans toward that kind of interpretation, and some key concepts, such as "union," "participation," and others, highlight the motifs of deification.

Simo Peura, who has written a full-scale monograph on the idea of deification in Luther,[41] shows that the idea of deification is an integral motif in Luther's theology. The most explicit passage comes from Luther's *Sermon on the day of St. Peter and St. Paul* (1519):

> For it is true that a man helped by grace is more than a man; indeed, the grace of God gives him the form of God and deifies him, so that even the Scriptures call him "God" and "God's son."[42]

Another example comes from Luther's Christmas sermon of 1514:

> Just as the word of God became flesh, so it is certainly also necessary that the flesh become word. For the word becomes flesh precisely so that the flesh may become word. In other words: God becomes man so that man may become God. Thus power becomes powerless so that weakness may become powerful. The logos puts on our form and manner.[43]

It is easy to see that Luther presents here, following Athanasius and Irenaeus, the idea of deification as a union of logos and flesh, or word and man. Even though the distinction between human and divine is not negated, the union is real, it is "a community of being of God and man."[44] According to Mannermaa, Luther did not understand the union as signifying any change of substance; yet for Luther the union

---

[40] The term "deification" in various forms (*deifico/vergotten/durchgotten*) appears 30 times in Luther's corpus. Simo Peura, "Vergöttlichungsgedanke in Luthers Theologie 1518–1519," in *Thesaurus Lutheri*, 171–72.

[41] Peura, *Mehr als ein Mensch?* For publications and discussion of the results of the Mannermaa school's research on deification, see *Luther und Theosis*, S. Peura and A. Raunio, eds. (Helsinki: Luther-Agricola Society, 1990); *Thesaurus Lutheri*, T. Mannermaa et al., ed. (Helsinki: Luther-Agricola-Society, 1987); *Luther und Ontologie*, Kari Kopperi et al., ed. (Helsinki: Luther-Agricola Society, 1993); *Nordiskt forum för studiet av Luther och luthersk teologi*, vol. 1, ed. T. Mannermaa [in German] (Helsinki: Luther-Agricola Society, 1993).

[42] *WA* 2, 247–48, LW 51, 58. Incidentally, it is from this passage that the title for Peura's work comes: *Mehr als ein Mensch*, "More Than a Man?"

[43] *WA* 1, 28, 25–32, quoted in Mannermaa, "Theosis," 43.

[44] Mannermaa, "Theosis," 44.

"does signify a community of being." This means that "just as the Logos not only 'took on our flesh' in the incarnation but 'really *is* flesh,' so 'we not only *have* the word in faith,' but we 'are it as well.'"[45]

Another way to look at the doctrine of justification and its parallels with the Eastern doctrine of *theosis* in Luther is to focus on Luther's doctrine of God. It is highly significant here that for Luther the divinity of the triune God consists in the reality that "God gives" himself. The essence of God, then, is identical with the essential divine properties in which he gives of himself, called the "names" of God: Word, justice, truth, wisdom, love, goodness, eternal life, and so forth. "The *theosis* of the believer is initiated when God bestows on the believer God's essential properties; that is, what God gives of himself to humans is nothing separate from God himself."[46] A Christian is saved when the "spiritual goods" or the names of God are given to her. God is, as Luther says, the whole beatitude of his saints; the name of God donates God's goodness, God himself, to the Christian; the spiritual goods are God's gifts in the Christian.[47] Not only is the human being saved when God gives himself to the Christian; in that very same act, God proves to be the real God when he donates his own being to humanity. "Thus, God realizes himself and his own nature when he gives his wisdom, goodness, virtue, beatitude, and all of his riches to the Christian, and when a Christian receives all that he gives."[48]

As already mentioned, although the term "deification" is not frequent in Luther, the core idea is integral; he usually prefers terms like "presence of Christ in faith," "participation in God," "union with God," *perichoresis,* the famous Eastern term, and others. Christ's real presence in a believer is the leading motif in Luther's soteriology. A classic formulation can be found, for example, in his *Lectures on Galatians* (1535). Speaking about "true faith," Luther says: "It takes hold of Christ in such a way that Christ is the object of faith, or rather not the object, but so to speak, the One who is present in the faith itself. . . . Therefore faith justifies because it takes hold of and possesses this treasure, the present Christ."[49]

[45] Mannermaa, "Why is Luther So Fascinating?" 11 (italics in the original) with reference to *WA* 1, 28, 25–32.

[46] Mannermaa, "Why is Luther So Fascinating?" 10; Peura, "Christ as Favor and Gift," 49–50.

[47] *WA* 3, 454, 4–10; 303, 20–26.

[48] Peura, "Christ as Favor and Gift," 50; *WA* 4, 278, 24–35.

[49] *WA* 40 I, 228–29; Saarinen, "The Presence of God," 5–6.

The idea of participation in Christ is related to this. The core of the doctrine of justification and deification from this viewpoint is the idea of real participation in the divine life in Christ. We receive the salvatory gifts through participation in Christ.[50] Luther does not hesitate to say that "we are born again into eternal life by faith, that we may live in God and with God and be one with him, as Christ says (John 17:21)."[51]

Faith unites with Christ and the believer becomes one with Christ. Through faith Christ dwells in the believer. The relationship between Christ and the believer could be compared to the bride-bridegroom union; they become "one flesh" according to Ephesians 5:29-30.[52] In fact, this means that in the moment of justification the believer participates in something that she lacks herself, namely the infinite righteousness of Christ.[53]

The idea of union and the consequent divinization becomes understandable also from the perspective of love. As we already noticed in the beginning of this chapter, Luther is a theologian of love.

> Love, according to its classic theological definition, is the power that unites the lover and the beloved to each other. Luther made this classic understanding of the nature of love his own. Both pure, unselfish, and impure, self-serving love are unifying powers. The Reformer often argues that pure love, as well as the faith through which such love is given, is the copula that unites God and the human heart to each other. God first loves man and becomes one with the object of his love. And then this love affects those who receive it in such a way that they begin as well as to love God. . . . The person thus partakes of God and thereby undergoes a thoroughgoing transformation. Love is a unifying power that tends to change the loving person into what is loved.[54]

Arto Seppänen summarizes this core idea of Luther's doctrine of justification in the following way:

> Through faith the Christian and Christ are one, the union of which is pictured in the union between a bride and bridegroom. On the basis of this union [literally: being one] the Christian possesses all that Christ has in the same way the bride has everything that belongs to her bridegroom.

---

[50] Cf. Wolfhart Pannenberg, *Systematic Theology*, vol. 3 (Grand Rapids, Mich.: Eerdmans, 1998) 215ff.

[51] WA 42, 48; Saarinen, "The Presence of God," 6–7.

[52] WA 2, 145, 18–20.

[53] Arto Seppänen, *Unio Christi: Union ja vanhurskauttamisen suhde Anders Nohrborgin postillassa*, Suomalaisen Teologisen Kirjallisuusseuran julkaisuja 211 (Helsinki: STKJ, 1997) 38.

[54] Peura, "What God Gives Man Receives," 81.

Similarly, the sins of the human being become Christ's possession. It is the *unio* which makes possible this participation. The whole of Christ is donated to the believer. The donation takes place through faith in Christ. "Happy exchange" is related to the essence of faith and is a natural consequence of the union with Christ.[55]

As "gift" *(donum)* Christ gives himself in a real way to the Christian to bring about her participation in the divine nature.[56] To emphasize the union between Christ and the Christian, Luther sometimes even borrows expressions from the mystics,[57] as in his reference to the Song of Songs in the Heidelberg Thesis 27.[58] To interpret this as a sign of an existential effect or the union of wills, as has been done in the neo-Protestant interpretation tradition, does not do justice to Luther's ontology. There is no doubt about the fact that occasionally Luther adopted mystical language. One of the crucial concepts of the mystical tradition is the term *raptus*, "being caught up" in Christ. "It means not only that a Christian is joined with Christ but that in this union he is transformed into the likeness of Christ."[59]

But now an important question arises in light of Luther's overall theology, namely, is this a theology of glory? In other words, talk about the divinization of the human being clearly begs the question of whether Luther's controlling theological idea, namely, the theology of the cross, has been surpassed. As we saw in the previous section, for Luther the nature of human existence is that of *nihil*, "nothing." Before God gives himself to a person in his Being—or as Luther often calls it, "Word," since these two mean the same thing—God names that person "empty" and "nothing." This "reducing to nothing" *(reductio in nihilum)* leads to agony and self-condemnation, in other words, to a real perception of oneself in light of the cross, which finally opens up the way to receive God's wonderful gifts. Even this work of annihilation, though, should be understood as a result of God's love. Its goal is the emergence of a new being and the destruction of false human love. Now, for a person who has been made form-less, in other words, "nothing," *(deformis),*

---

[55] Seppänen, *Unio Christi*, 37 (my trans.).

[56] Mannermaa, *In ipsa fide Christus adest: Luterilaisen ja ortodoksisen kristinuskonkäsityksen leikkauspiste*, 24–26.

[57] For the disputed question of the role of the mystical in Luther, see Franceen Neufel, "The Cross of the Living Lord: The Theology of the Cross and Mysticism," *Scottish Journal of Theology* 49, no. 2 (1996) 131–46.

[58] *HDT* 27; *LW* 31, 57.

[59] See further, Peura, "Christ as Favor and Gift," 60; see further 60–63 with texts from Luther.

God gives a new form, "in-forms" him to an image of Christ.[60] Christ as the "greatest sinner"—Luther also uses the concept of "Christ as the only sinner"[61]—in a "happy exchange," gives himself to us to make it possible for us to participate in him.[62]

For Luther, participation in Christ, following Paul (Phil 3 et al.) is also participation in his cross. Furthermore, we could express this same truth by using still another favorite expression in Luther, namely, "hidden under its opposite." Luther's understanding of the doctrine of revelation is totally governed by the idea of God revealing himself by hiding himself. In other words, God lets the human being see something of himself, yet at the same time, conceals himself and his goods under its opposites. As already mentioned, this same paradox applies to the Christian life in general, including the doctrine of participation in Christ. "The participation that is a real part of his theology is hidden under its opposite, the *passio* through which one is emptied. It is not grasped in rational knowledge but only in faith, and the grasp that faith has of it in this life is still on the beginning of a much greater participation that awaits in eschatological fulfillment."[63]

Thus, for Luther, the idea of deification is closely linked with his theology of the cross and the theology of love. Clearly, the organizing principle of Luther's theology is his theology of love and the related concept of the cross. The doctrine of salvation forms an integral part of that whole theological outlook.

In order to further analyze the distinctive nature of Luther's understanding of salvation and justification and its relation to divinization, vis-à-vis the differing interpretation of later Lutheranism, the concept of "grace" and "gift" have to be looked at in detail. To that topic we now turn.

4. Christ as Favor and Gift: The Relationship Between Effective and Forensic Justification

Traditionally, it has been claimed that the most distinctive feature of the Lutheran doctrine of justification is the forensic imputation of Christ's righteousness to the believer through faith. Forensic justification has

[60] Kopperi, *Paradoksien teologia,* 148–49. See further *WA* 56 [The Exposition of Romans] 218, 17–219.
[61] Mannermaa, "Justification and *Theosis* in Lutheran-Orthodox Perspective," 31.
[62] Ibid., 29–36.
[63] Mannermaa, "Why is Luther So Fascinating?" 10.

become the hallmark of Lutheranism so much so that according to the standard textbook views, this is what distinguishes Lutheranism from Catholicism. Supposedly, effective justification, in other words the view according to which the believer is not only proclaimed just but also made just, is typical of the Catholic understanding, whereas forensic justification is typical of Lutheran theology. Also, with regard to Orthodox-Lutheran conversations, there is usually an assumption that the Eastern concept of *theosis* represents an actual change, not unlike the supposedly Catholic theology of effective justification, whereas the Lutheran notion is opposed to that.

Simo Peura, one of the ecumenical researchers on Luther in the Mannermaa School, therefore, says bluntly: "We Lutherans will encounter great difficulties if we try to represent only the forensic aspect of justification."[64] No wonder, that for recent ecumenical Luther scholarship one of the most difficult problems to be solved concerns the relation between the forensic and the effective aspects of justification. It also has bearing upon the question of Lutheran identity. At the same time, this question relates to the difficult problem of the relationship between Luther's own theology and the theology of Lutheran confessions to which we referred in the beginning of this chapter. There is no denying the fact that here Lutheranism differs significantly from Luther. The basic rule can be stated as follows: For Luther himself, the forensic and effective aspects of justification form an indivisible entity, while for the Lutheran confessions and later Lutheran theology these two aspects are distinguished from each other.[65]

The relationship between effective and forensic justification comes to light in Luther's theology in his usage of two classic concepts: "grace" *(gratia, favor)* and "gift" *(donum)*. The former denotes the sinner's being declared righteous (the forensic aspect) and the latter the person's being made righteous (the effective aspect). As early as the beginning of Luther's career, in his *Lectures on Romans* (1515–1516), this distinction appears. Following the terminology of Augustine and the Medieval tradition, on the basis of Romans 5:15 *(gratia Dei et donum in gratia)*, Luther expresses an opinion that is totally in line with the mainline Catholic teaching, but which has been lost sight of in later Lutheranism: "But

[64] Simo Peura, "Christ as Favor and Gift," 42, n. 1.

[65] In the following exposition, I am heavily dependent especially to Simo Peura, "Christ as Favor and Gift," 42–69 and "Christus als Gunst und Gabe: Luthers Verständnis der Rechtfertigung als Herausforderung und den ökumenischen Dialog mit der Römisch-katholischen Kirche," in *Caritas Dei,* 340–63.

'the grace of God' and the 'gift' are the same thing, namely, the very righteousness which is freely given to us through Christ."[66] In other words, Luther found it most important already in these early years to relate grace and gift closely to each other, and to understand them both as given to the Christian through Christ. Thus we can see that grace and gift together constitute the donated righteousness of a Christian.

According to Peura, "grace and gift are given not only through Christ, but in Christ and with Christ. For whatever distinction Luther makes between them, he always keeps them together." In other words, grace and gift are in Christ and are given to us when "Christ is 'poured' into us."[67] As Luther puts it: "Grace actually means God's favor, or the good will which in himself he bears toward us, by which he is disposed to pour Christ and the Holy Spirit with his gifts into us."[68] Luther also teaches that the gospel gives the sinner two goods to oppose two evils, namely the wrath of God and the corruption of the Christian: grace and gift.[69]

For Luther, the distinction between effective and forensic righteousness is not an issue, as it has been in subsequent Lutheran doctrine. What is crucial to Luther's own doctrine of justification is the distinction between two kinds of righteousness, namely the righteousness of Christ and the righteousness of the human being.[70] The first type Luther defines in the following way: this is the alien righteousness which is being infused to us from outside; it is that kind of righteousness that Christ is in himself and it is the righteousness of faith. It is this righteousness of Christ that makes the human being just.[71]

Furthermore, Luther states that this first type of righteousness is being given without our own works solely on the basis of grace.[72] This is the famous *sola gratia*. Human activity is totally excluded in this process. The infusion of this first kind of righteousness is more than mere forensic imputation, it also means the realization of the righteousness of Christ in the believer. In other words, this first kind of righteousness brings about the union between Christ and the believer. The term "union" is one of the most important catchwords for Luther and also ties closely with his idea of deification, as we have seen above.

[66] WA 56, 318, 28–29; LW 25, 306.
[67] Peura, "Christ as Favor and Gift," 43.
[68] WA DB 7, 9, 10-14 quoted in Peura, "Christ as Favor and Gift," 43.
[69] Peura, "Christ as Favor and Gift," 43.
[70] In this section I am indebted to the careful exposition of Seppanen, *Union ja vanhurskauttamisen suhde*, 32–55.
[71] WA 2, 145, 9–14.
[72] WA 2, 146, 29–30.

The other kind of righteousness is given righteousness, in this sense human righteousness. Luther calls it "our" righteousness.[73] It is a result of the first kind of righteousness and makes it effective, "perfects" it.[74] Even though it is called "our" righteousness, its origin and source is outside the human being, in the righteousness of Christ. Christ's righteousness is the foundation, cause, and origin of human righteousness.[75] Christ present in faith "absorbs all sin in a moment," since the righteousness of Christ infused into the human heart is "infinite"; still, the power of sin and death is deteriorating day by day, and this process continues until death.[76] The infusion of Christ's righteousness into the heart of the believer means the beginning of the process of nullifying the power of sin and transforming fallen nature. The emerging good deeds have nothing to do with salvation, for the believer is already justified, and the only purpose of the good deeds now is the good of other people.[77]

In other words, for Luther the forensic imputation of Christ's righteousness is not the key to his view of justification. Rather, the key is Christ present in faith and the consequent union; as a result of Christ's righteousness, the believer will become one with Christ. This fact also explains the unity between sanctification and justification in Luther: they both belong to the sphere of the righteousness of Christ infused into the heart of the believer by faith. It is an "alien" righteousness in the sense that its origin and source is outside the human being, but it is a "present" righteousness in the sense that it becomes the possession of the human being. This present righteousness in the form of Christ's presence is the power for sanctification and transformation. Luther even goes so far as to say that the victory over sin takes place only in Christ's body and in his person.[78]

By his understanding of grace, Luther wants to emphasize the importance of Christ's person for our salvation. The expression "grace of Christ" "refers to Christ's personal grace, because he among all people is the only one who is in God's judgment favorable and acceptable. While Christ's person is acceptable to God, the merciful God manifests his favor to Christ. This means that God favors all of Christ's deeds as well. So, everything Christ has done for our salvation is good and favorable

[73] *WA* 2, 146, 36.
[74] *WA* 2, 147, 12–13.
[75] *WA* 2, 146, 16–17.
[76] *WA* 2, 146, 12–16, 32–35.
[77] *WA* 2, 146, 36–147, 33.
[78] *WA* 40 I, 433, 26–434, 14.

in God's judgment.[79] Furthermore, for Luther Christ's person and the grace and gift earned on the cross cannot be separated. As Peura expresses it, Christ is not only the necessary means of grace but "he is in himself full of grace and gift (John 1:14). Thus, it is Christ himself who has become grace and gift for sinners."[80]

> Grace is the external good that opposes the greater evil, God's wrath. Grace is God's mercy *(misericordia Dei)* and favor *(favor Dei)*. This favorable and friendly attitude toward the sinner is an attitue that God has in himself. When God shows his grace, a sinner encounters not a hostile God but a merciful and favorable God. God's favor effects in the sinner a conviction that God is gracious, and his conscience becomes joyful, secure, and fearless. According to Luther, then, grace is God's favorable mood effecting in a sinner confidence in God's forgiveness and benevolence. Furthermore, grace is by its nature always comprehensive: either God is favorable toward a sinner or he is not. Gift, however, constitutes the Christian's internal good, and it opposes his internal evil, that is, the corruption of human nature. Gift means righteousness *(iustitia)* and faith of/in Christ *(fides Christi)*. It is donated with the purpose of conquering the sin *(concupiscentia)* that remains as a corruption of the Christian's human nature. Gift effects in a sinner his real renewal *(renovatio)*, because it replaces sin with the righteousness of Christ and purifies a sinner from sin *(sanitas iustitiae)*.[81]

Now the difference between Luther's own theology and the theology of the Lutheran confessions becomes clear when we look more carefully at how they understand the relationship between forensic and effective righteousness, in other words, the relationship between grace and gift. The Formula of Concord (FC) teaches that the doctrine of justification includes only God's favor which means imputed or forensic justification. Peura summarizes this understanding of justification in the following way:

> Justification is the same as absolution, the declared forgiveness of sin. The imputation of Christ's obedience to us has the effect of changing the position of the sinner *coram Deo*. One is accepted as a child of God and as an inheritor of eternal life. Contrary to Luther, however, the FC excludes gift, the renewal of a Christian and the removal of sin, from the doctrine *(locus)* of justification. The FC indeed mentions gift, but at the same time it defines the gift in a radically limited sense compared with Luther. The gift is faith: the right knowledge of Christ, confidence in him, and the se-

---

[79] Peura, "Christ as Favor and Gift," 52.
[80] Ibid., 52–53.
[81] Ibid., 44; see also 43.

curity that God the Father consider us righteous because of the obedience of Christ. So, gift means in the FC only the reception of forgiveness,
knowledge of faith, and confidence *(fiducia)*, a gift that I would call a
donum minimum.[82]

What makes this view of the Lutheran confessions so radically different from Luther and Catholic theology is that the meaning of "gift" is
minimized and that the essential aspects of effective righteousness,
such as regeneration, renewal, vivification, and God's presence in the
sinner are excluded from the doctrine of justification. These become
consequences of God's forensic action in which he declares the sinner
righteous. The Formula of Concord explicitly says that the indwelling
of God is not that righteousness by which we are declared righteous.
The indwelling of God, rather, follows the antecedent justification by
faith. This means that God is not really present in the Christian when
declaring her righteous through faith for Christ's sake.[83]

The motive behind the Formula of Concord opposing the indwelling
of God was its rejection of Andreas Osiander, who emphasized the indwelling of the divine nature in his doctrine of justification. However,
what was at stake with Osiander was not his doctrine of justification
but his truncated Christology; he separated Christ's human and divine
natures and made the human nature's role in redemption and the death
of Christ instrumental and subsidiary.[84]

Lutheran theologians have since followed the understanding of the
confessional books according to which grace and gift are separated and
focus has been laid on the forensic aspect. Philosophically this was aided
by the rise of neo-Kantianism, which follows Immanuel Kant in separating God's being and God's effects. In this scheme, the only thing we can
know are the effects of God on the believer. All kinds of ontological specu-
lations into the "essence" of things are rejected, and so understandably
the idea of the "real" presence of Christ in the believer or of the union between God and the human being is totally foreign. Consequently, gift and
the effective aspect of justification have lost their ontological content. Gift
has taken on the meaning of a new revelation of God, a change in one's
self-understanding of existential confidence in God's mercy. The content

[82] Ibid., 45, with reference to FC, Solid Declaration, III, 10–11.
[83] Ibid., 45.
[84] Simo Peura, "Gott und Mensch in der Unio: Die Unterschiede im Rechtfertigung-
sverständnis bei Osiander und Luther," in *Unio: Gott und Mensch in der nachreformatorischen Theologie*, Matti Repo and Rainer Vinke, eds. (Helsinki: Luther-Agricola-Gesellschaft
35, 1996) 33–61.

of gift is actually reduced to the Christian's insight that he has a new position *coram Deo*.[85] Simo Peura summarizes the implications:

> Even if this conviction is the most important existentially for a Christian,
> since he can then trust in God's favor, it actually means that the effective
> aspect of justification is reduced to something that happens only intrinsi-
> cally in the human mind, in awareness, and in knowledge. The renewal
> of the sinner is a consequence of one's new relation to God. When a Chris-
> tian has become aware of forgiveness and finds himself freed from the
> punishment for sin, his mood changes and he begins to do good works
> toward others.[86]

Ecumenically this means that to reduce the doctrine of justification
either to a forensic declaration or a new self-awareness, the Lutheran
understanding of justification is viewed in opposition to both the Catholic and Orthodox positions, and also to later Free Church soteriologies
with their emphasis on sanctification and the change in one's life. A
good example of this is Rudolf Herrmann's (1846–1922) analysis of
Luther's concept of gift. Herrmann worries about the possibility that
Luther's view might correspond to the Catholic understanding according to which the renewed Christian is covered by a supernatural gift.[87]

The conclusion of the Mannermaa School with regard to the differences between Luther's theology and the theology of the Lutheran confessions and subsequent Lutheranism is well worth hearing because of
its profound ecumenical implications:

> the FC [Formula of Concord] and modern Lutheran theology have not
> correctly communicated Luther's view of grace and gift . . . justification
> includes gift in its broader sense, that is, in its effective aspect as the re-
> newal of the sinner *(renovatio)*. This aspect belongs integrally to Luther's
> view of justification, and it is not a mere consequence of forensic imputa-
> tion. Justification is not a change of self-understanding, a new relation to
> God, or a new ethos of love. God changes the sinner ontologically in the
> sense that he or she participates in God and in his divine nature, being
> made righteous and "a god."[88]

This interpretation is based on the thesis that both grace and gift are
a righteousness given in Christ to a Christian. This donation presupposes

[85] Peura, "Christ as Favor and Gift," 46.
[86] Ibid., 46–47.
[87] Rudolf Herrmann, *Luthers These "Gerecht und Sunder Vergleich"* (Gütersloh, 1960)
108–9, 280; Peura, "Christ as Favor and Gift," 47.
[88] Peura, "Christ as Favor and Gift," 47–48.

that Christ is really present and that he indwells the Christian. Christ on the one hand is the grace that is given to the sinner that protects him against the wrath of God (the forensic aspect), and on the other hand he is the gift that renews and makes the sinner righteous (the effective aspect). All this is possible only if Christ is united with the sinner through the sinner's faith. So, the crucial point of this interpretation rests in the notion of *unio cum Christo*, "union with Christ."

5. The Christian as "Christ" to the Neighbor

Further insight into the distinctive nature of Luther's theology of justification may be gained from looking at the implications of Christ's presence in the believer for her transformation and her behavior and attitudes toward other people. Luther's understanding of the nature of God's love and his view of the real presence of Christ in the believer opens up the horizon into his understanding of neighbor love. Insofar as the relationship to God is no longer based on human love in which there is a movement towards God, but rather is based on the reception of God's love in faith, works of love are released to serve the needs of other people.[89]

Luther's main thesis is daring: As a result of the presence of Christ, the Christian becomes a "work of Christ," and even more a "Christ" to the neighbor.[90] In other words, the Christian does what Christ does. This is, in other words, *in ipsa fide Christus adest*, the real presence of Christ in the believer. The presence of Christ for Luther is not only "spiritual" or external *(extra nos)* but rather real and "internal" *(in nobis)*.[91] In fact, Luther says, then he is "one with us"[92] and that "Christ lives in us through faith."[93] Now, "since Christ lives in us through faith . . . he arouses us to do good works through that living faith in his work, for the works which he does are the fulfillment of the commands of God given us through faith."[94] For example, as Christ, the Christian identifies with the suffering of her neighbor.[95]

[89] The main work here is Raunio, *Die Summe des christlichen Lebens*.

[90] For the notion of the Christian as a "Christ" to the neighbor, see Mannermaa, *Kaksi rakkautta*, 89–100.

[91] Mannermaa, "Uskon ja rakkauden suhde Lutherin teologiassa," *Teologinen Aikakauskirja* 84 (1979) 332–33; Peura, *Mehr als ein Mensch*, 270–94 especially.

[92] *HDT* 26; *LW* 31, 56.

[93] *HDT* 27; *LW* 31, 56.

[94] *HDT* 27; *LW* 31, 56–57.

[95] Kopperi, *Paradoksien teologia*, 154ff.

We can certainly do nothing for our salvation, but our neighbors need our work, that is, our love: Every man is created and born for the sake of others.[96] For if I do not use everything that I have to serve my neighbor, I rob him of what I owe him according to God's will. Luther sometimes describes the essence of sin as "robbery of God."[97]

> All works except for faith have to be directed to the neighbor. For God does not require of us any works with regard to himself, only faith through Christ. That is more than enough for him; that is the right way to give honor to God as God, who is gracious, merciful, wise and truthful. Thereafter, think nothing else than that you do to your neighbor as Christ has done to you. Let all your work and all your life be turned to your neighbor. Seek the poor, sick, and all kinds of wretched people; render your help to those; surrender your life in various kinds of exercises. Let those who really need you enjoy you, insofar as it is possible with regard to your body, possessions, and honor.[98]

Justification for Luther means primarily participation in God through the indwelling of Christ in the heart through the Spirit. Through faith, a human being also participates in the characteristics of God, or as Luther often says, of the Word of God. On the one hand, this participation means putting down those human traits that are contrary to the righteousness of God, and on the other hand, participating in the goodness, wisdom, truthfulness, and other characteristics of God. Luther also expresses this truth by saying that God in fact becomes truthful, good, and just in the person when God himself makes the person truthful, good, and just. Never is there reason to boast, though, since even the presence of Christ and its consequences are always hidden in the Christian.[99]

According to its very nature, God's love is overflowing, seeking objects not worthy in themselves to be loved: "This is the love of the cross, born of the cross, which turns in the direction where it does not find good which it may enjoy, but where it may confer good upon the bad and needy person. . . . Therefore, sinners are attractive because they are loved; they are not loved because they are attractive."[100] The theology of glory seeks God in heaven, in glory—and thus it errs in its object. Paul Althaus has commented on this: "Our faith is not to seek God's deity in heaven but in the humanity of Christ; the same is true of

---

[96] *WA* 21, 346.
[97] *LW* 32, 224.
[98] *WA* 10 I, 2, 168, 18–26 (Advent Postil, 1522, my trans.).
[99] Raunio, *Summe des Christlichen Lebens*, 172–77 especially.
[100] *HDT* 28; *LW* 31, 57.

our love. Since God has become man, our love for God should show it-self as love for men. God is very close to us, that is, in men. This is true no less of our love than for our faith. Thus Luther's understanding of love is completely dominated by his faith in the incarnation."[101]

For Luther the golden rule, "So in everything, do to others what you would have them do to you" (Matt 7:12 NIV), is both a natural law and the principle of Scripture.[102] As a natural law, it is also a spiritual law. "As natural and spiritual law it is the origin of all other laws."[103] As such, the golden rule is the guiding principle of our relationship both to God and to other persons. The requirement of the golden rule with regard to God means giving God all the honor and praise that God deserves and wills, in other words, returning to God that which the fallen human nature wants to rob of God. Thereafter the human being is ready to give the neighbor what she also wants herself.[104]

For a human being it is not possible to fulfill the requirements of the law. Christ is the one who fulfills the law;[105] all the commandments of the Second Tablet are to be found in love:

> Love is the common virtue of all virtues, their fulfillment and source. Love feeds, gives drink, clothes, consoles, prays, makes free, helps, and saves. What do we say then? It gives itself, body and life, possessions and honor and all its power internally and externally to meet the desperate need of the neighbor for his benefit. It does not hold back anything either from a friend or fiend with which it can serve other people. Therefore, no virtue can be compared to it, neither is it possible to describe or name any specific work for it as with regard to other virtues, which are actually partial virtues, such as purity, charity, patience, and goodwill, etc. Love

---

[101] P. Althaus, *The Theology of Martin Luther*, Robert C. Schultz, trans. (Philadelphia: Fortress, 1966) 133–34.

[102] Raunio, *Summe des Christlichen Lebens*, 129–33 especially. Luther notes that even in the animal world a principle of mutuality like this holds. *WA* 4, 593, 4–8.

[103] Raunio, *Summe des Christlichen Lebens*, 146 (my trans.). Raunio (147) reminds us of the fact that, against many earlier interpretations, Luther does not make a distinction be-tween a "worldly natural law" *(weltliches Naturgesetz)* and a divine law of love *(göttliches Gesetz der Liebe)* but rather "the natural law is the spiritual law." For English synopsis, see Raunio, "Natural Law and Faith: The Forgotten Foundations of Ethics in Luther's Theol-ogy," in *Union with Christ*, 96–124.

[104] Raunio, *Summe des christlichen Lebens*, 154; 161–63. "Robbery" of God means, on the contrary, wishing to keep for oneself the honor and praise and all the good things due to God (154–55).

[105] Ibid., 252–85 includes a very detailed study of the meaning of the golden rule in relation to the Ten Commandments.

does everything . . . so much so that Saint Paul says that all the commandments are included in this summa: love your neighbor.[106]

Luther's understanding of God's love and love toward neighbor also has important ecclesiological implications. Since Christians are living in the world they are involved with people who are sinful and less than perfect; therefore, the church of Christ in the world cannot be anything other than a hospital for the incurably sick. The *summa* of the Christian life is to bear the burden of one's neighbor. Consequently, the task of the bishops and pastors is to act as if their dioceses were a hospital and their church members were sick in need of medical treatment:

> This is the *summa* of the Gospel: The kingdom of Christ is a kingdom of mercy and grace. It is nothing else than continuous bearing of [each other's] burdens. Christ bears our wretchedness and sicknesses. Our sins he will take upon himself and he is patient when we are going astray. Even now and forever he carries us on his shoulders and never tires of carrying us. . . . The task of the preachers in this kingdom is to console consciences, associate in a friendly spirit with the people, feed them with the nourishment of the Gospel, carry the weak, heal the sick, and take care of everybody according to their need. That is also the proper ministry for every bishop and pastor.[107]

Luther also describes the interesting dialectic between Christian as "lord" and "servant" at the same time. On the one hand, as a result of the presence of Christ, the Christian is "above all" and on the other hand "under all." Through faith the spirit of the Christian is taken into the heights of God, but at the same time that she is being elevated, she should also do what God's love always does, namely orient oneself downward, to that which is nothing in itself. Consequently, the Christian is both totally free and totally bound by the needs of others. She is totally free and totally given to service to others.[108]

6. The Pneumatological Potential of Luther's Doctrine of Salvation

> I believe that by my own understanding or strength I cannot believe in Jesus Christ my Lord or come to him, but instead the Holy Spirit has called me through the gospel, enlightened me with his gifts, made me holy and kept me in the true faith. . . .[109]

---

[106] *WA* 17 II, 100, 26–101,4 (*Lent Postil*, 1525, my trans.); see also *WA* 17 II, 95, 17–24.

[107] *WA* 10 I-II; 366, 18–34 (*Summer Postil*, 1526, my trans.).

[108] Raunio, *Summe des christlichen Lebens*, 179–81.

[109] Martin Luther, *Small Catechism* in *The Book of Concord*, R. Kolb and T. Wengert, eds. (Minneapolis: Fortress Press, 2000) 355.

Generally speaking, Reformation theology viewed faith as the decisive work of the Holy Spirit, as the quote above from Luther clearly shows. Luther's exposition of the third article of the Creed in the 1531 Small Catechism understands faith as a gift of the Holy Spirit.[110] However, the later development of Reformation soteriology, especially in the Lutheran tradition, came to be expressed more in christological than in pneumatological terms. In the Latin Middle Ages, there was a close relation between pneumatology and the doctrine of grace, though most medieval theologians did not equate the Holy Spirit with the gift of love *(caritas)* poured into our hearts, but distinguished this gift of grace as a *gratia creata*, "the created grace" from the Holy Spirit himself. In Calvin's theology in general and his soteriology in particular, the pneumatological orientation was preserved more carefully.

It is a general consensus of the most recent Luther scholarship that the commonly held forensic doctrine of justification by faith as articulated by later confessional writings, under the leadership of Melanchthon, is a one-sided understanding of Luther's theology, and it blurs the meaning of the Holy Spirit in salvation. Luther himself speaks of the real presence of God in Christ and the Holy Spirit in the believer, as we have seen.[111] So it is understandable that the pneumatological potential of Luther's theology has come to light along with the findings of this new perspective on Luther. An important impetus to the recovery of a pneumatological outlook in the doctrine of salvation for Lutherans has, understandably, come from contacts with Eastern Orthodox theology, a tradition that is pneumatologically pregnant.

Pneumatological implications of this new approach of Luther scholarship are obvious. The leading idea, Christ present through faith, can also be expressed pneumatically: it is through the Spirit of Christ that the mediation of salvatory gifts is accomplished. Participation in God is possible only through the Spirit of Christ, the Spirit of adoption. "There is no justification by faith without the Holy Spirit. Justifying faith is itself the experience that the love of God has been poured into our hearts 'through the Holy Spirit' (Rom 5:5)."[112]

Deification is, of course, a pneumatologically loaded image of salvation. The pneumatological orientation was acknowledged early in Lutheran-Orthodox conversations. Defining "the new road leading to de-

[110] See Wolfhart Pannenberg, op. cit., vol. 3, 2.

[111] Cf. the highly interesting article by the Lutheran Kenneth L. Bakken, "Holy Spirit and Theosis: Toward a Lutheran Theology of Healing," *St. Vladimir's Theological Quarterly* 38, no. 4 (1994) 409.

[112] Ibid., 410.

ification" as a "process of growing in holiness," the joint document cites two important Pauline texts: "But we all, with open face beholding as in a mirror the glory of the Lord, are changed into the same image from glory to glory, even as by the Spirit of the Lord" (2 Cor 3:18). Deification takes place under the influence of the grace of the Holy Spirit by a deep and sincere faith, together with hope and permeated by love (1 Cor 13:13).[113]

Several major research projects at the University of Helsinki currently underway are focusing on pneumatological orientations in Luther.[114] The title of Miikka Ruokanen's preliminary study clearly expresses its purpose: *Spiritus vel gratia est ipsa fide* (Spirit or grace is the faith itself), with the subtitle, *A Pneumatological Concept of Grace in Luther's De servo arbitrio*.[115] Contrary to what is usually thought of Luther's major work *De servo arbitrio* (in which he vehemently attacks Erasmus), Ruokanen argues that the theology of grace and justification is conceived very much in terms of pneumatology. Ruokanen shows that Augustine's concept of pneumatological *gratia increata* (i.e., the personal presence of the triune God in man through the Holy Spirit) might be the indispensable theological background for Luther's emerging pneumatology of grace.

Ruokanen very carefully distinguishes Luther's theology of grace in *De servo arbitrio* both from the Scholastic and Nominalistic *(via moderna)* doctrines of grace, and shows that there is a direct link in Luther's doctrine of grace with Augustine's pneumatological understanding of grace. In distinction from Eastern theology—and Luther's understanding of Erasmus—Luther places *liberium arbitrium* (free will) against the gracious effect of the Holy Spirit; this is in line with Luther's concept of necessity. Luther also strongly opposes the Scholastic rule *facientibus quod in se est Deus non denegat gratiam suam* (to those who do what they can God does not deny his grace).

Luther's theology centers on the person and the work of Christ, and its modes of thought are christologically concentrated. But Ruokanen shows that in *De servo arbitrio* even Luther's theology of the cross takes a profoundly pneumatological form; "it is still the same *gratia increata*

[113] Hannu Kamppuri, ed., *Dialogue between Neighbours, The Theological Conversations between the Evangelical-Lutheran Church of Finland and the Russian Orthodox Church 1970–1986* (Helsinki: Luther-Agricola Society, 1986) 75.

[114] The classic introduction to Luther's pneumatology is Regin Prenter, *Spiritus Creator,* John M. Jensen, trans. (Philadelphia: Muhlenberg Press, 1953). See also V.-M. Kärkkäinen, *Pneumatology: A Contemporary Introduction* (Grand Rapids: Baker Academic Books, 2002) 79–87.

[115] Still in an unpublished version (University of Helsinki, 1991, 124 pp.). It is expected that Prof. Ruokanen will expand it to a monograph, to be published both in Finnish and English. Hereafter referred to as *Spiritus vel gratia est ipsa fide.*

of the merciful God who makes a sinner just by presenting the sinner
the righteousness of Christ."[116] Holding to the classical canon according
to which the works of the Trinity are indivisible externally, it is possible
for Luther to create a doctrine of justification in terms of pneumatology.
Interestingly enough, Ruokanen argues that adhering to pneumatology
is the means by which Luther can completely refute all the synergistic
tendencies implied by the *facere quod in se est* axiom of the Nominalists.
For Luther, pneumatology represents divine initiative, "God's moner-
gism," distinct from and in contrast to any notion of the natural capacities of the human will.[117]

According to Ruokanen, the Holy Spirit, the Spirit of Christ, is the
living divine reality which encounters man and woman and creates a
mystical unity between the sinner and the Holy Trinity.

> The Holy Spirit makes the outcome of Christ's crucifixion and resurrec-
> tion an instant and intimate reality which enters the intimate center of
> human personality and touches the ultimate limits and foundations of a
> person's life and existence.[118]

In line with his anthropology, Luther's doctrine of grace is sharp-
ened by his strong conception of the opposing spiritual powers. He emphasizes that no neutrality exists: either God's Spirit vivifies the human
being, or she lives in the enslavement of the powerful enemy. The central place of pneumatology in the doctrine of justification safeguards
the idea of the absolute freedom and mercifulness of the divine Almighty.
The Holy Spirit is the agent of movement and change. No other entity
can be substituted for the third person of the Holy Trinity.[119]

Ruokanen summarizes his study by saying that grace for Luther is
the personal presence of Christ or the Holy Spirit in the inmost secrecy
of the human being.[120]

Another highly interesting study concerning the pneumatological implications of Luther's theology in general and the doctrine of salvation in
particular is the interpretation of the doctrine of salvation in charismatic
Lutheran theology. Markku Antola has recently published his dissertation,
which analyzes the main doctrinal document of this renewal movement.[121]

---

[116] Ruokanen, *Spiritus vel gratia est ipsa fide,* 108.
[117] Ibid., 108–9.
[118] Ibid., 109–10.
[119] Ibid., 110.
[120] Ibid., 111.
[121] Markku Antola, *The Experience of Christ's Real Presence in Faith: An Analysis of the Christ-Presence-Motif in the Lutheran Charismatic Renewal,* Schriften der Luther-Agricola-

The charismatic theology of Lutheranism describes charismatic experience as the presence of the Triune God through his Spirit.[122] The actual purpose of the Holy Spirit's work is to create faith in Christ and lead the believer into a "living union" with Christ. "But the Holy Spirit alone creates true faith, whereby one is actually united with the living Christ as the present and redeeming Lord."[123] It is noteworthy that Christ's presence is often expressed by the union with Christ concept:

> "If any one is in Christ, he is a new creation" (2 Cor 5:17). The newness is not simply the fact that human nature has been forgiven and cleansed. . . . The newness goes deeper: a person now lives in union with the risen Christ. That which has been created, the 'new creation,' is precisely this reality of the indwelling Spirit establishing and maintaining the risen Christ and the believer in a living union.[124]

Explicitly using Luther's language, the charismatic theology maintains that "in the faith itself Christ is present."[125] Also, "Faith describes the whole action by which the Holy Spirit brings the living, redeeming presence of Christ into a living union with a human being. The initiative and the power to accomplish this lies with the Spirit."[126]

Also, in line with Luther's own theology—but not necessarily subsequent Lutheranism—charismatic theologians teach that the forgiveness of sins and the imputation of Christ's work to the believer (*favor Dei*) cannot be separated from *unio* with Christ, where Christ comes to live in the believer as God's gift (*donum*). In other words, justification not only includes God's favor but also Christ as the gift living in the Christian.[127] The charismatic Lutheran theology is also helpful in maintaining that—in line with Luther himself, but against his later interpreters—justification and sanctification, rather than being two distinct matters, occur alongside each other and happen simultaneously.[128]

Gesellschaft 43 (Helsinki: Luther-Agricola-Society, 1998). The primary source of the study was the International Lutheran Charismatic Renewal Leaders' Consultation from 1982–1985, published as *Welcome Holy Spirit,* Larry Christenson, ed. (Minneapolis: Augsburg, 1987).

[122] Antola, op. cit., ch. 2, "The Charismatic Experience as the Presence of God," especially 53ff.

[123] Christenson, op. cit., 141.

[124] Christenson, op. cit., 142; Antola, op. cit., 56–57.

[125] Christenson, op. cit., 142–43; Antola, op. cit., 58.

[126] Christenson, op. cit., 69.

[127] Antola, op. cit., 58.

[128] Ibid., 64.

The pneumatological orientation of Luther's theology comes to the fore in an important quotation that the soteriological document of the Renewal Movement cites from Luther. It speaks about the integral connection between the Spirit and experience, a theme that sounds foreign to many observers of Lutheranism but which is not necessarily so in light of Luther's own theology:

> No one can correctly understand God or his Word unless he has received such understanding immediately from the Holy Spirit. But no one can receive it from the Holy Spirit without experiencing, proving, and feeling it.[129]

Ecumenically, it is highly significant that the role of the Spirit in the doctrine of salvation is gaining more and more ground as is evident, for example, in the Lutheran Wolfhart Pannenberg's recent *Systematic Theology*. The main section on soteriology is entitled, "The Basic Saving Works of the Spirit in Individual Christians." Pannenberg's main thesis argues that "The Holy Spirit is the medium of the immediacy of individual Christians to God as he lifts them up to participation in the sonship of Jesus Christ and grants them, as a permanent gift, the Christian freedom that enables them to call confidently on God as 'our Father' (Rom 8:15)."[130]

Before delving into the contemporary dialogues between Lutherans, Orthodox, and Roman Catholics, a brief survey and assessment of the understanding of salvation in so-called "free churches" is in order. It is typical of theological textbooks and monographs to ignore contributions from "the margins." Yet, in terms of numbers, free churches represent the fastest growing segment of Christianity. In order to advance the ecumenical quest for a common understanding of salvation, I will here relate free church insights to Lutheran, Orthodox, and Roman Catholic views. This is a task that I hope will receive greater attention in future ecumenical research.

---

[129] Christenson, op. cit., 117–18; Antola, op. cit., 61. Ecumenically this statement is important since it brings to light the same emphasis that has even been characteristic of a more recent Catholic doctrine of grace. Karl Rahner, the most noted spokesperson for the new approach, against the widespread Neo-scholastic position that grace cannot be experienced (because it is supernatural), holds that people do experience grace. Following Rahner, several leading theologians of the Catholic church have come to describe the essence of grace and salvation in pneumatological terms. For a detailed discussion, with bibliographical references, see Veli-Matti Kärkkäinen, *Spiritus ubi vult spirat: Pneumatology in Roman Catholic-Pentecostal Dialogue 1972–1989*, Schriften der Luther-Agricola-Gesellschaft 42 (Helsinki: Luther-Agricola-Society, 1998) 160ff.

[130] Pannenberg, op. cit., vol. 3, 134.

5

Deification, Union, and Sanctification in Later Protestant Theologies

1. Deification in Anabaptism

Church history, as any other history, is written from the perspective of those who hold power. Even at the end of the nineteenth century, most church historians still divided Western Christianity into Protestant and Catholic types without remainder. A whole array of legitimate Christian churches and communities were left out. These were mainly the descendants of the radical Reformation. Anabaptism and later Baptist movements were on the one hand forerunners of later free Churches and on the other hand the legacy of that part of the Protestant Reformation that wanted to go further than the magisterial reformers went.[1] Radical reformers were dissatisfied with the "compromises" of their mainline counterparts and wanted to take the "reformation" to its end.[2] Anabaptism was the pioneer of these left-wingers. "Anabaptism" has two established meanings. First, it refers to the sixteenth-century movement of the Radical Reformation. Second, when used more broadly, it indicates Anabaptism's Mennonite descendants, though many of the

---

[1] See further, James Wm. McClendon Jr., *Doctrine: Systematic Theology*, vol. 2 (Nashville: Abingdon Press, 1994); see also John J. Kiwiet, "Anabaptist Views of the Church," in Paul Basden and David S. Dockery, *The People of God: Essays on the Believers' Church* (Nashville: Broadman Press, 1991) 225–34.

[2] Michael Novak, "The Free Churches and the Roman Church: The Conception of the Church in Anabaptism and in Roman Catholicism: Past and Present," *Journal of Ecumenical Studies* 2 (1965) 429.

same features characterize the later Hutterite and Amish movements, as well as the Society of Friends and the Church of the Brethren.

The doctrine—and practice—of salvation, understandably, was in the forefront of such a radical reformation vision. One of the earliest statements of the Radical Reformation, the Pilgrim Marpecki of 1545, said that: "the church of Christ—inwardly of spiritual quality, and outwardly as a body before the world—consists of men born of God. They bear in their cleansed flesh and blood the sonship of God in the unity of the Holy Spirit which has cleansed minds and dispositions." Therefore, the difference between the apostolic church and the compromised state church, as they saw it, was shocking. "First and fundamental . . . was the conception of the essence of Christianity as discipleship." This "meant the transformation of the entire way of life of the individual believer and of society . . . fashioned after the teaching and example of Christ."[3]

According to the classic study of Ernst Troeltsch, Anabaptists and Spiritualists translated the radical implications of *sola fide* into a practical lifestyle and everyday religion without cultus.[4] Anabaptists, as well as their successors, focused on sanctification much more than the Reformers, even to the point of being accused by Reformers of "salvation by works." Later revivalistic movements inherited from Anabaptists and Spiritualists an intensive eschatological awareness coupled with the emphasis on the Holy Spirit's transforming power. Thus, the Anabaptist focus was not so much the inward experience of the grace of God but "the outward application of that grace to all human conduct and the consequent Christianization of all human relationships."[5]

Thomas Finger, a Mennonite theologian who has compared Eastern Orthodox theology with Anabaptism, maintains that in the left wing of the Reformation the idea of deification was no stranger and that it was sometimes enthusiastically embraced. Finger maintains that Anabaptism can be seen as a sixteenth-century expression of an ascetic impulse originating in Eastern cenobitic monasticism. Another Mennonite scholar, Kenneth Davis, similarly argues that Anabaptism arose primarily from Christianity's ascetic stream, chiefly expressed in monasticism, stretching back to the first centuries. Asceticism involved the

[3] Harold S. Bender, "The Anabaptist Vision," *Mennonite Quarterly Review* 18 (April 1944) 67.

[4] Ernst Troeltsch, *Protestantism and Progress: A Historical Study of the Relation of Protestantism to the Modern World*, W. Montgomery, trans. (Philadelphia: Fortress, 1986, orig. 1912); Thomas Finger, "Anabaptism and Eastern Orthodoxy: Some Unexpected Similarities," *Journal of Ecumenical Studies* 31 (1994) 69, 70.

[5] Bender, op. cit., 79.

struggle against fallen, fleshly impulses and separation from "worldly" society. Positively, it consisted in a striving for transformation by Christ-like virtues, or holiness. Though asceticism, according to Davis, was often intertwined with mysticism, Davis asserts that renewal in character and conduct, rather than simply in knowledge or experience, was the goal of asceticism.[6]

Finger points to evidence that for these persecuted people, the doctrine of *theosis* brought hope and encouragement.[7] He lists a host of Mennonite leaders, such as Hans Denck, Melchior Hofmann, Menno Simons, and others who championed the idea of divinization.[8] For example, Denck claimed that the Divine Word existed in every person's depth "that it might divinize them."[9] Another Anabaptist Leonhard Schiemer asserted that if he fully knew God on the basis of Christ as our righteousness, his "spirit and soul would be so overjoyed that this joy would penetrate into the body and it would become unfeeling, impassible, immortal, and glorified."[10]

However, at the outset, one may wonder if any kind of convergence between two so radically different Christian traditions would ever be possible:

> Few religious communions would seem more distant than Eastern Orthodoxy and Anabaptists. While the former claims millions of adherents and a history of nearly two millennia, the latter, a relatively small movement, originated at the time of the Reformation. While an elaborate sacramental and liturgical life grounds the former, diversity and informality have marked the latter in such matters. And, while Orthodoxy has helped guide great world empires, Anabaptists have usually rejected participation in the state.[11]

In line with Eastern Christians, but in contrast to the Reformers, Anabaptists understood grace as a transforming divine energy.[12]

[6] Kenneth Davis, *Anabaptism and Asceticism: A Study in Intellectual Origins* (Scottdale, Penn.: Herald Press, 1974) 37–38.
[7] Finger, "Anabaptism and Eastern Orthodoxy," 67–91.
[8] Thomas Finger, "Post-Chalcedonian Christology: Some Reflections on Oriental Orthodox Christology from a Mennonite Perspective," in *Christ in East and West*, Paul Fries and Tiran Nersoyan, eds. (Macon, Ga.: Mercer University Press, 1987) 162.
[9] Cited in Finger, "Anabaptism and Eastern Orthodoxy," 78.
[10] Cited in Ibid., 79.
[11] Ibid., 67.
[12] Ibid., 76, on the basis of Alvin J. Beach, *The Concept of Grace in the Radical Reformation*, Biblioteca Humanistica & Reformatorica 17 (Nieuwkoop, The Netherlands: B. DeGraaf, 1977).

According to the groundbreaking research of Alvin J. Beach, grace brings about "a reversal of the incarnation in which the eternal Word becomes man in order that man may become God."[13] The Swiss Anabaptist theologian Balthasar Hubmaier often characterized redemption as rebirth through the Spirit.[14] Similarly, among South German/Austrian Anabaptists, clear references to divinization abound; the same can be said of the Hutterites of the same area, as well as of the Dutch Anabaptists.[15]

Anabaptists developed their own distinctive view of the *imago Dei*. For them, the "language of renewal, re-creation, and restoration of humanity in the image of God is a powerful way to speak of salvation as the possibility of a radically new life in the midst of the old."[16] For example, Peter Riedeman said, "Therefore faith is a real divine power, which renews man and makes him like God in nature, makes him living in his righteousness, and ardent in love, and in keeping his commandments."[17]

It is amazing how Eastern sounds the text from Dirk Phillips, a colleague of Menno Simons:

> All believers are participants of the divine nature, yes, and are called gods and children of the Most High . . . they yet do not become identical in nature and person itself to what God and Christ are. Oh, no! The creature will never become the Creator and the fleshly will never become the eternal Spirit itself which God is. . . . But the believers become gods and children of the most high through the new birth, participation, and fellowship of the divine nature.[18]

J. A. Osterhuus makes a highly interesting ecumenical claim that whereas Catholicism considered grace an accident of the human soul, bestowed in somewhat mechanical fashion, and the Reformers considered it a divine activity, yet one making little direct contact with the human, for the Dutch Anabaptists, grace played a far more comprehensive role: it was the divine energy underlying creation, incarnation, and

---

[13] Beach, op. cit., 71.

[14] H. Wayne Pipkin and John H. Yoder, *Balthasar Hubmaier: Theologian of Anabaptism*, Classics of the Radical Reformation 5 (Scottdale, Penn. and Kitchener, Ont.: Herald Press, 1989) 100, 147, 238 especially.

[15] Evidence, with original sources, to be found in Finger, "Anabaptism and Eastern Orthodoxy," 78–79 and 81–83 respectively.

[16] C. Norman Kraus, *Jesus Christ Our Lord: Christology from a Disciple's Perspective*, rev. ed. (Scottdale, Penn.: Herald Press, 1990 [orig. 1987]), 194.

[17] Cited in Kraus, *Jesus Christ Our Lord*, 194–95.

[18] Cornelius J. Dyck; William E. Keeney; and William A. Beachy, *The Writings of Dirk Philips, 1504–1568*, Classics of the Radical Reformation 6 (Scottdale, Penn. and Waterloo, Ont.: Herald Press, 1992) 145–46, quoted in Finger, "Anabaptism and Eastern Orthodoxy," 81.

sanctification.[19] Even if this caricature might not do full justice to either Catholic or Reformed soteriology, the convergence of the Anabaptist view of grace with the Eastern soteriology is startling.

As mentioned above, eschatological fervency has been typical of Anabaptism since its beginnings. Finger contends that we can see here yet another commonality between Anabaptism and Eastern Orthodoxy. Like most Reformers, Anabaptists believed that history's end was already breaking in. Like many earlier and later apocalyptical revivalist movements, Anabaptists could not help but devise their own time-tables for the return of Christ. Even where these failed, Anabaptists believed they had rediscovered the eschatological nearness in which the true church had always lived and was to live until the end. According to the Orthodox theological vision, the church relates to the world chiefly as bearer of and witness to the eschatological reality, with all the tension this involves. A sense of the eschatological "already" envelops the liturgy, where Christ's "forthcoming advent is already realized, and 'time' is being transcended."[20] Finally, the goal of the Christian life in the Eastern view is the "mystical encounter . . . an authentic present experience of final participation in God."[21]

Notwithstanding some methodological questions (e.g., the linkage, if any, between sixteenth-century Anabaptism and Eastern Orthodoxy[22]), enough evidence shows clear convergences between these early free church theologies and the Eastern view of salvation. How much of this convergence is due to the similarity of language only cannot be determined in the confines of this study. What these commonalities do show, however, is that the Radical Reformation on the one hand wanted to preserve a revivalist spiritual dynamic with separation from the world and sin, and on the other hand, in its insistence to "go back to sources"— both the Bible and the vibrancy of the early centuries before the "great compromise" of the state church—cherished the ancient Christian desire

---

[19] J. A. Oosterbaan, "Grace in Dutch Mennonite Theology," in *A Legacy of Faith: The Heritage of Menno Simons*, Cornelius J. Dyck, ed. Mennonite Historical Series (Newton, Kans.: Faith and Life, 1962) 69–85.

[20] John Meyendorff, *Byzantine Theology: Historical Trends and Doctrinal Themes*, 2nd ed. (New York: Fordham University Press, 1979) 219; see also Alexander Schmemann, *Church, World, Mission: Reflections on Orthodoxy in the West* (Crestwood, N.Y.: St. Vladimir's Seminary Press, 1979) 10, 48–49.

[21] Vladimir Lossky, *The Vision of God* (Crestwood, N.Y.: St. Vladimir's Seminary Press, 1983) 145–46.

[22] Finger in "Anabaptism and Eastern Orthodoxy," 68, seems to be aware of the limitations of his line of questioning in terms of methodology.

for total devotedness to and union with God. Mere intellectual faith or legal change of one's status before God was hardly enough for these enthusiasts. The doctrine of salvation was depicted in dynamic, life-changing, transformative terms with holiness and sanctification being the ultimate focus. How these ideas that, of course, resonate with much of early Christianity both in the East and West came to be reappropriated in later times can be seen in our discussion of the soteriological foci of Wesleyanism, a spiritual successor to both the magisterial and radical reformation.

2. Deification and Sanctification in Methodism

On the morning of his Aldersgate experience in 1738, when his heart was "strangely warmed," John Wesley, the spiritual and theological architect of the diverse group of holiness revivalist traditions, was incidentally reading 2 Peter 1:4, "whereby are given to us exceeding great and precious promises that by these ye might be partakers of the divine nature." The powerful spiritual experience that sprang from his hunger for a deeper, more intimate relationship with God resulted in a form of spirituality that bears surprisingly close resemblance to many aspects of the Eastern Orthodox tradition. Consequently, Wesley's vision of the Christian life was "empowered by an optimism of grace, not by the threat of judgment; it is a gospel which sees the fulfillment of God's purposes not in the redemption of humankind alone but in the redemption of the whole creation."[23]

Even though this unprecedented spiritual and theological connection between Methodism/holiness movements and Eastern Orthodox spirituality has caught the attention of several scholars only very recently, it was in the 1960s when Albert Outler detected this relationship, although first in a sidenote.[24] His initial finding was that Wesley's doctrine of sanctification was directly influenced by his exposure to the *Spiritual Homilies* attributed to Macarius of Egypt (but actually written by a fifth-century Syrian monk under the theological influence of Gregory of Nyssa). Even some Orthodox theologians such as Charles Ashanin

[23] A. M. Allchin, "The Epworth-Canterbury-Constantinople Axis," *Wesleyan Theological Journal* 26, no. 1 (Spring 1991) 35.

[24] Albert C. Outler, *John Wesley*, Library of Protestant Thought 1 (New York: Oxford University Press, 1964) 9–10, n. 26. See also his "John Wesley's Interest in the Early Fathers of the Church," *Bulletin of the United Church of Canada Committee on Archives and History* 29, no. 2 (1980) 5–17.

have pointed out that the classical Methodist doctrine of sanctification "is probably Wesley's adaptation of the Patristic doctrine of Theosis."[25] These kinds of findings have led Wesleyan scholars to wonder where to place Wesley theologically: is he a "Westerner" or more appropriately located in the Eastern Christian tradition?[26]

Themes such as the goal of the Christian life as perfected love,[27] the role of the Holy Spirit in the entire sanctification of the Christian's life,[28] and the emphasis on Christian virtue[29] resonate directly with Eastern Orthodox emphases. They are indications of the general orientation of the Wesleyan doctrine of salvation; not the "pardoning" but "participation" is the key to the Christian life and salvation, in other words, union with God in perfect love and holiness.[30] Thus, Wesley "urge[s] a divine-human communion, a coinhering communion which extends far beyond the moment of conversion."[31] The following passage from one of his sermons from the earlier part of his ministry encapsulates this strong Eastern motif of union and *theosis:*

> "The desire of thy soul shall be to his name"—is none other than this. The one perfect good shall be your ultimate end. One thing shall ye desire for its own sake—the fruition of him that is all in all. One happiness shall ye propose to your souls, even an union with him that made them, the having fellowship with the Father and the Son, the being "joined to the Lord in one Spirit." One design ye are to pursue to the end of time— the enjoyment of God in time and in eternity. Desire other things so far as they tend to this. Love the creature—as it leads to the Creator. But in every step you take be this the glorious point that terminates your view. Let every affection, and desire or fear, whatever ye seek or shun, whatever ye

[25] Charles Ashanin, *Essays on Orthodox Christianity and Church History* (Indianapolis: Broad Ripple, 1990) 90.

[26] For the recent discussion, see K. Steve McCormick, "Theosis in Chrysostom and Wesley: An Eastern Paradigm on Faith and Love," *Wesleyan Theological Journal,* 26, no. 1 (Spring 1991) 40–44.

[27] See further, W. Stanley Johnson, "Christian Perfection as Love for God," *Wesleyan Theological Journal* 18, no. 1 (Spring 1993) 50–60.

[28] See further, William M. Arnett, "The Role of the Holy Spirit in Entire Sanctification in the Writings of John Wesley," *Wesleyan Theological Journal* 14, no. 2 (Fall 1979) 15–30.

[29] See further, David Bundy, "Christian Virtue: John Wesley and the Alexandrian Tradition," *Wesleyan Theological Journal* 26, no. 1 (Spring 1991) 139–55.

[30] See further, A. C. Outler, "The Place of Wesley in the Christian Tradition," in *The Place of Wesley in the Christian Tradition,* Kenneth E. Rowe, ed. (Metuchen, N.J.: Scarecrow Press, 1976) 29–32.

[31] Edmund J. Rybarczyk, *Beyond Salvation: An Analysis of the Doctrine of Christian Transformation Comparing Eastern Orthodoxy with Classical Pentecostalism,* Fuller Theological Seminary, Ph.D. dissertation (1999) 15.

think, speak, or do, be it in order to your happiness in God, the sole end
as well as source of your being. Have no end, no ultimate end, but God.
Thus our Lord: "One thing needful."[32]

Wesley drew from the well of Eastern spirituality in his readings of
the Eastern fathers' spiritual texts; in fact, he preferred the Eastern
teachers over the Westerners.[33] These included Athanasius, Basil, John
Chrysostom, Clement of Alexandria, Clement of Rome, Dionysius the
Areopagite, Gregory of Nazianzus, Ephraem Syrus, Origen, and others.[34] There is no doubt that Wesley owes to the early Greek fathers the
development of both his own anthropological understanding and the
ensuing experientially oriented doctrine of entire sanctification often
called perfection.[35] However, it has to be noted that Wesley himself did
not, of course, regard himself as in any way an Eastern Orthodox spir-
itualist. Moreover, it is doubtful how much he would have been willing
to account for that influence; like any Western revivalist of that time, he
was very critical of several features of the Eastern church and abhorred,
for example, its rigid liturgy as he saw it.

However, Wesley learned so many spiritual lessons from the Eastern fathers, for example from Clement of Alexandria that there are
three kinds of persons: the unconverted, the converted but immature,
and the mature or perfect Christian. Each required spiritual instruction
appropriate to his or her state. Clement's three principal works *(Prop-
treptikos, Paidagogos, Stromateis)* address these three classes of persons.
In John and Charles Wesley's *Hymns and Sacred Poems* (1739), a poem is
titled "On Clement Alexandrians' Description of a Perfect Christian."
This is but one concrete example how this Eastern taxonomy of Christian spiritual development was adopted by Wesleyanism.[36]

[32] John Wesley, *The Bicentennial Edition of the Works of John Wesley,* F. Baker, ed.
(Nashville: Abingdon Press, 1984) 1:408.
[33] See further, Michael J. Christensen, "Theosis and Sanctification: John Wesley's Re-
formulation of a Patristic Doctrine," *Wesleyan Theological Journal* 31, no. 2 (Fall 1996) 71–94.
[34] See further, Ted A. Campbell, *John Wesley and Christian Antiquity* (Nashville:
Kingswood Books, 1991) appendix 2, 125–34; for this note I am indebted to Edmund J.
Rybarczyk, op. cit., 12 n. 25. See also T. A. Campbell, "Wesley's Use of the Church Fathers," *The Asbury Theological Journal* 50, no. 2 (Fall 1995) 47–51, and (Spring 1996) 60.
[35] For argumentation, see Randy Maddox, "John Wesley and Eastern Orthodoxy: Influences, Convergences and Divergences," *Asbury Theological Journal* 45, no. 2 (1990) 29–53.
I am well aware that the notion of "perfection" or "entire sanctification" is a debated
issue in Wesleyan studies as to its precise meaning. In the confines of this brief ecumenical exposition mainly of Wesley's own theology, the details of that debate cannot be discussed.
[36] See further, Michael J. Christensen, op. cit., 76–77.

This kind of taxonomy, of course, sets his theology in tension with the standard Protestant view of justification. Wesley, of course, knew the category of "justification," and as an inheritor of Protestant Reformation, Anglican, and especially Pietistic spiritualities and theologies, he gave due attention to it. Even though his own spiritual journey was not marked by anything desperate like that of Luther's—for Wesley the agony was over the "deeper life" rather than guilt as such—the emphasis on entire sanctification and perfection led him to highlight the importance of pardoning and being justified, too. But, together with his experiential emphasis, Wesley preferred to center the Christian life around sanctification rather than justification.[37] In this insistence on the need for a real transformation of the believer's life, Wesley not only approaches the ethos of the Eastern Orthodox tradition but also that part of Western spirituality that has been marked by Roman Catholic theology.

For the Roman Catholic tradition, as will become evident in the discussion on the Council of Trent's view of justification and later Catholic formulations, emphasis shifts from justification to sanctification. We also need to take into account the fact that Wesley was raised in Anglicanism, the form of spirituality that is in many ways much closer to Catholicism than magisterial Protestantism. Finally, what makes Wesley and his contribution so fascinating is that he was really a product of so many Christian traditions: Puritanism, Anglicanism, Lutheranism by way of Moravian Pietism, Roman Catholicism, and Eastern Orthodoxy by way of the Eastern fathers. What marks his approach, however, is not only a creative adaptation of various influences but also critique and honest wrestling with seemingly conflicting tendencies.[38]

It is interesting to note how Wesley as the leading champion of modern Protestant revivalist traditions ended up cherishing the kind of spiritual exercises that have always been treasured dearly in both Eastern and Western mystical and spiritualistic traditions such as monasticism. The life of sanctification, the goal of which is perfect union with God, involved ascetic activities and disciplines such as fasting on Wednesdays, Fridays, and the prescribed days of the ancient church, attending catechetical classes, and penance. Moreover, those disciplines were necessary for all Christians, not just the clergy. Since the Greek fathers practiced asceticism, and since, in Wesley's opinion, they so clearly

[37] For a careful, balanced assessment, see Maddox, "John Wesley and Eastern Orthodoxy," 39.
[38] See further, Theodore Runyon, "New Creation: A Wesleyan Distinctive," *Wesleyan Theological Journal* 31, no. 2 (Fall 1996) 6.

lived out a life of Christian holiness, he, in turn, encouraged ascetic activities as a way to repristinate eighteenth-century British and American Christianity. Asceticism aided believers in the restoration of the original image of God which, in Wesley's theology, had been lost in the fall. "Like the ancient Greek Christian ascetics, Wesley believed that the soul's therapy could be facilitated through ascetic cures."[39]

So, the Christian life was not just a matter of judicial pardon, although human beings certainly needed that. Because human beings were marred and corrupted, Christ had also come to restore the image of God in humanity. In the words of Alexander Knox, the colleague of John Wesley:

> But what has John Wesley done? In my mind, in a manner unprecedented, he has not overlooked the forgiveness of sins, but he has, indeed, looked much above it, and beyond it. . . . The faith, therefore, which my friend urged his hearers to implore from God, had not one great fact only for its object. It did not merely relate to the propitiation of our sins, but it was an influential, vital apprehension of all the Divine facts which are placed before us in the Gospel.[40]

John Wesley was open to the idea of deification and to a pneumatological understanding of the concept of grace. Wesley discerned five stages in the sanctification of life from an awakening of the conscience by a preliminary divine grace to a gradual sanctification of life to the final stage: "Believers are wholly interpenetrated by the Holy Spirit and arrive at the state of Christian perfection, the *theosis*."[41]

Jürgen Moltmann correctly notes that for Wesley sin is a sickness that requires healing rather than a breach of law requiring atonement. Therefore, Wesley was less interested than Reformation theology in the permanent justification of the sinner and more interested in the process of a moral renewal.[42] Ted Campbell has even argued that Wesley regarded the Gospel as a "medicine," a cure. The result was that Wesley "developed something like a scientific taxonomy of spiritual problems" which his own Methodist ministers could diagnose and cure.[43]

[39] Rybarczyk, op. cit., 13; see also Campbell, "Wesley's Use of the Church Fathers," 62–66.

[40] Alexander Knox, *Remains of Alexander Knox, Esq.* (London: Duncan and Malcom, 1844) 3:162–64; for this reference, I am indebted to Rybarczyk, "Beyond Salvation," 14, n. 36.

[41] Jürgen Moltmann, *Spirit of Life: A Universal Affirmation* (Minneapolis: Fortress Press, 1992) 165, with ample references to both Wesley's original works and his interpreters' works. For a helpful discussion, see also K. Steve McCormick, "Theosis in Chrysostom and Wesley: An Eastern Paradigm on Faith and Love," *Wesleyan Theological Journal* 26, no. 1 (Spring 1991) 44–48.

[42] Moltmann, *Spirit of Life*, 164.

[43] Campbell, "Wesley's Use of the Church Fathers," 65.

By participating in the life of grace, a life given by the Holy Spirit, the Christian is enabled to love God, other people, and the whole of creation with a perfect love. It is noteworthy that for Wesley this vision of the transformation of life not only encompassed individual life but also the whole creation—another indication of similar orientations between the East and Wesley. In fact, for Wesley the category of "new creation" combined in a critical way both individual and cosmic aspects of salvation. His was a vision of the very real transformation in the creature and the world that salvation brings about. "The note of hope and expected transformation virtually sings its way through many of the sermons produced by Wesley during the final years of his long life."[44] The following passage from his 1783 sermon "The General Spread of the Gospel" echoes this hope in a most beautiful way:

> [God] is already renewing the face of the earth: And we have strong reason to hope that the work he hath begun, he will carry on unto the day of the Lord Jesus; that he will never intermit this blessed work of his Spirit, until he has fulfilled all his promises; until he hath put a period to sin, and misery, and infirmity, and death; and re-established universal holiness and happiness, and caused all the inhabitants of the earth to sing together, "Hallelujah, the Lord God omnipotent reigneth!"[45]

As is clearly visible in this passage, the new creation is cosmic in its overall dimensions and implications, but is focused for Wesley in the renewal of persons. "Ye know that the great end of religion is to renew our heart in the image of God," he proclaimed.[46] The renewing of the face of the earth begins, therefore, with the renewing of its human inhabitants. This is the pattern followed by the Eastern fathers, linking cosmic redemption to human salvation.

This vision of a new creation also reminds us of the close link between the doctrine of creation in Luther and his view of love, both divine love and human. Even though Luther took the problem of guilt more seriously than either Eastern theology or Wesley, Luther never tired of highlighting the all-important role of God the Father as the provider of all good things, which are displayed in creation. Loving God means loving not only other human beings created in the image of God but also the rest of God's good creation. Finally, God's transforming

---

[44] Runyon, op. cit., 6; I am indebted to Runyon's insightful article (5–19) for the following exposition and references.

[45] John Wesley, *Works*, vol. 2:499.

[46] Ibid., 2:185.

power will effect the purification of all the cosmos. Even though Luther did not say it so explicitly, his theology is pregnant with this vision. The distinctive feature that sets the Wesleyan approach apart from the predominant Protestant heritage, even though not necessarily Luther's own views, however, is Wesley's insistence that the renewal of the image of God involves the creature in actual transformation—in no less than re-creation; it is a "real" as well as "relative" change in the believer.[47] Here we find a debate between the interpreters of Wesley. Often it is claimed that the idea of entire sanctification or perfection in Wesleyanism differs from the Eastern idea of *theosis*, in that whereas the Greek fathers tended to describe this deification in ontological terms, Wesley preferred to describe this transformation using affective terms.[48]

The distinction between "relative" and "real" change goes back to Wesley's distinctive understanding of the relationship between justification and sanctification. Wesley connects justification with "relative" change in the believer; but to correctly understand the meaning of the term *relative* here one has to notice that Wesley uses the term in its literal sense, meaning "relational" or "being in relation to." In other words, justification effects the change in the nature of the relationship between the sinner and God. In justifying us God sets us in a new relationship, which is basic to everything that follows. The *relative* change lays the foundation for a *real* change in the creature, and it is this real change that brings about the renewal of the image of God and which is the ultimate goal of salvation.[49]

Theodore Runyon has made the interesting observation that Wesley's view of the *imago Dei* has a clear resemblance to the tradition of the Eastern fathers. In an early sermon Wesley described human beings as receiving the love of God and then reflecting that love toward all other creatures. The image of God, then, was viewed not as a human capability or inherent possession, but as a living relationship made possible by divine grace. In this he shared the understanding of the image found in the Eastern fathers who used the metaphor of humanity as a "mirror," called not only to mirror God in their lives, but to reflect into the world the grace that they receive, and thus to mediate the life of God to the rest of creation.[50]

[47] Cf. Runyon, op. cit., 7.

[48] So Rybarczyk, op. cit., 13, with reference to Maddox, "John Wesley and Eastern Orthodoxy," 40.

[49] See further, Runyon, op. cit., 10–11 especially.

[50] Ibid., 8; Runyon makes reference to John Meyendorff, *A Study of Gregory Palamas* (London: Faith Press, 1964) 120.

Consequently, the image of God for Wesley was a vocation to which human beings are called, the fulfillment of which constitutes their true destiny. It resides not so much in the creature as in the way the creature lives out his or her relationship to the Creator, using whatever gifts and capacities have been received to be in communion with and to reflect God in the world. For this, the human person has been endowed with liberty and freedom of will, "a power of directing his own affections and actions, a capacity of determining himself, of choosing good or evil."[51]

Wesley's creative way of combining individual and cosmic aspects of salvation in his vision for perfect union between human beings and God has obvious social implications, too:

> Wesleyans are united, therefore, in insisting that salvation includes the transformation of the creature. Many would extend this transformation not only to the individual but to society. They find a peculiar affinity between Wesley's doctrine of sanctification and movements for social change. When Christian perfection becomes the goal on the individual level, a fundamental hope is engendered that the future can surpass the present. A holy dissatisfaction is aroused with regard to any present state of affairs— a dissatisfaction that supplies the critical edge necessary to keep the process of individual transformation moving. Moreover, this holy dissatisfaction is *readily transferable* from the realm of the individual to that of society, where it provides a persistent motivation for reform in the light of "a more perfect way" that transcends any status quo.[52]

To conclude our discussion of the idea of union and its implications in Wesleyan theology vis-à-vis Eastern Orthodoxy, it is fruitful to take a brief look at the relationship between the Wesleyan doctrine of sanctification and the Roman Catholic understanding. The Methodist John E. Culp has recently suggested that an ecumenical common point between Wesleyanism and Roman Catholicism could be found in the correlation of the Catholic notion of "supernatural" and Wesley's notion of sanctification. The term "supernatural," apart from popular usage in which it means something in contrast to "natural," is a technical term in the Catholic theological vocabulary going back to the Medieval period. For Thomas Aquinas, the word denoted divine presence. Modern Catholic theology, building on that basis, holds that supernatural means the presence of God in "nature," in the natural realm. In other words, supernatural does not mean something in opposition to the natural, but almost the opposite.

[51] Runyon, op. cit., 8.
[52] Ibid., 12, with reference to Runyon, ed., *Sanctification and Liberation* (Nashville: Abingdon Press, 1981) 10.

It is important to note that especially in the modern Catholic view the doctrine of the supernatural occurs in the context of the Holy Spirit's activity in human existence, and it comes to the fore in sanctifying grace. This is the thrust of the theology of Karl Rahner, the most influential post-conciliar Catholic thinker. This line of reasoning connects modern Catholic theology with the theology of the Eastern fathers. The central theme of the Roman Catholic doctrine of the supernatural is that human existence achieves its ultimate goal of deification through God's presence in the realm of the human. The goal of human existence is God.[53] The sanctifying grace in the power of the Spirit makes us finally godlike, "godded," which effects union with God. The Holy Spirit as God's free self-communication (Rahner) makes this union possible.[54]

The similarities of Wesley's vision of perfect union with God to both the Eastern Orthodox idea of deification and the Roman Catholic notion of supernatural are obvious here. They share the common foundational conviction that human existence is capable of becoming godlike. This occurs through human response to a contact initiated by God which culminates in a fully restored relationship with God and the transformation from human to godlike existence. In Roman Catholic doctrine the presence of the supernatural makes it possible for human existence to achieve its goal. In Wesleyanism, the notion of entire sanctification describes the possibility of a person loving God perfectly in response to God's love and grace, which makes possible the overcoming of the presence of sin in the believer's life. "The doctrine of sanctification expresses the ideal of being Godlike in love."[55] Both traditions also hold that even though divine action is absolutely necessary, human action is crucial in becoming godlike. The Roman Catholic doctrine of supernatural emphasizes this both by speaking of the divinization of human existence and by denying that this divinization is identification; divinization in the Catholic no more than in the Orthodox form does not mean the end of human existence but rather a call for human persons to see God as God is. Likewise, the Wesleyan doctrine of sanctification maintains a crucial role for human existence. Sanctification involves the human response to divine grace. Wesley, as do also all the Eastern teachers, reminds us of the fact that God does not sanctify apart from the believer's commitment to living the life worthy of God's call-

---

[53] Henri de Lubac, *The Mystery of the Supernatural* (New York: Herder & Herder, 1967) 149.
[54] See further, John E. Culp, "Supernatural and Sanctification: Comparison of Roman Catholic and Wesleyan Views," *Wesleyan Theological Journal* 31, no. 2 (Fall 1996) 149–53.
[55] Ibid., 159–60 (160).

ing.[56] Affinities such as these have made some Wesleyan scholars call Wesley an "evangelical catholic."[57]

3. Union in Evangelical Theology

The term *evangelical* in its current usage possesses at its best several different meanings and at its worst is being used as an almost sectarian defensive weapon. In its original meaning, "evangelical" denoted Protestant theology as opposed to Catholic theology; thus, for example the "Evangelical Lutheran Church" or "evangelical theological faculty." Another meaning was added in the twentieth-century English-speaking world, mainly in the United States of America but also in Great Britain. Now it denotes those Protestants who adhere to a more orthodox version of Christianity as opposed to the liberal left wing. Thus, there arose an "evangelical doctrine of Scripture" that holds the Word of God to be divine in its origin and trustworthy in all regards. In recent decades, the Evangelical Movement, which is transdenominational and global, representing not only all sorts of Protestants from Lutherans to Presbyterians to Baptists to Pentecostals but also Anglicans, has distanced itself from the more reactionary Fundamentalism, even though most Fundamentalists regard themselves as "true" Evangelicals. The latest development of the term has been the emergence of "Evangelical Catholics," a group of Christians who decided to stay in their mother church but adopted several doctrinal convictions not unlike those of their Roman Catholic counterparts. My reference to "Evangelical theology" here follows the main usage in the English-speaking world, namely various (mainly Protestant) Christian traditions who are open to the dialogue with all other Christians and want to cherish classical Christianity as explicated in the creeds and mainstream confessions, yet also remain open to the latest developments in theology and other academic fields.

A significant camp in Evangelical theology, especially its more conservative side, has tended to defend the classical Protestant doctrine of justification as over against the Roman Catholic version which, in their interpretation, tends to blur the distinction between justification and sanctification and thus open the door to "works righteousness." They have also been more critical of the developments in New Testament studies with regard to a reinterpretation of the term "justification" (and

---

[56] Ibid., 160–61. Culp is also well aware of the differences between these two concepts, "supernatural" and "sanctification"; that discussion is not necessary nor feasible.

[57] Outler, *John Wesley*, viii.

"righteousness"). Both defensive postures seem to stem from a similar motivation: for example, if, following E. P. Sanders and others, it can be shown that the Reformation interpretation of "the righteousness of faith" is not legitimate, they see the bulwark of the "faith alone" (or "grace alone") paradigm as endangered. An illustrative example is the view of the New Testament theologian D. A. Carson. First, he gives evidence that the recent Roman Catholic theology of justification has not made any substantial changes from the time of the Council of Trent in the sixteenth century and that, consequently, rather than highlighting personal faith, Catholicism still champions an "instrumental/causal" and sacramental understanding of salvation. Rather than being clear on forensic or declarative justification, which is the critical test of orthodoxy for these Evangelicals, the Catholic view of justification is deemed as "distributive" and semi-Pelagian.[58] These right-wing Evangelicals also want to make a clear distinction between justification and sanctification, the former being the cause and the latter its effect. Understandably, these Christians have also been extremely critical of the recent *Joint Declaration on the Doctrine of Justification* between Lutherans and Roman Catholics (1999). Finally, it has to be noted that for these Evangelicals, the issue of justification has a significance that goes far beyond soteriological matters; it touches the core of their identity and beliefs. Carson expresses this clearly:

> For many evangelicals, for example, our understanding of justification is tied to a rejection of purgatory, indulgences, and claims that Mary may properly be called a coredemptrix. For us the doctrine of purgatory (to go no farther) implicitly asserts that the death of Christ on the cross for sinners was in itself insufficient or inadequate. Catholics, within a quite different framework, draw no such conclusion.[59]

These more conservatively-minded Evangelicals have also understandably been much more cautious about the Eastern Church's idea of salvation as union. Don Fairbairn in his rather conciliar exposition of the Eastern doctrine of *theosis* from an Evangelical perspective comes to the conclusion that what makes Eastern soteriology so problematic is that the emphasis falls on the "process of spiritual growth" and it "does not even include the idea of being declared righteous at the beginning of faith, an idea which is pivotal to virtually all evangelical thought."[60]

---

[58] D. A. Carson, "Reflections on Salvation and Justification in the New Testament," *Journal of the Evangelical Theological Society* 40, no. 4 (1997) 598–602 especially.

[59] Ibid., 604.

[60] Don Fairbairn, "Salvation as *Theosis*: The Teaching of Eastern Orthodoxy," *Themelios* 23, no. 3 (1998) 46. Fairbairn's critique focuses on the views of the Orthodox Maximos

Fairbairn argues that for Westerners, the issue of a person's status before God is one of the most critical of all questions. In contrast, the question hardly surfaces for Easterners, given the central place of the concept of *theosis*. That, according to him, makes these two soteriologies so different.[61] Fairbairn further contends that by eliminating the dividing line between justification and sanctification, the Eastern doctrine of salvation simply becomes unacceptable to Evangelicals. Then he adds a most provocative and bold thesis: "From our perspective, justification (as God's declaration that a sinner is righteous) is not simply a Western idea whose origin lies in our legal way of viewing reality. We are convinced that this is a biblical idea, indeed, one of the most central of all biblical truths."[62] Not unlike their Western Catholic counterparts, the Eastern theologians are accused of failing to stress the nature of salvation as a free gift. "Orthodox doctrine is likely to impact people by giving them a sense that they need to perfect themselves in order to have complete communion with God."[63]

In other words, both of these examples of "evangelical" critiques of the Western Roman Catholic and the Eastern Orthodox doctrines of salvation, one coming from the United States and the other from England, actually treat one type of Protestant interpretation of justification as *the* test of orthodoxy. This is the view of the Lutheran confessions in the way Melanchthon and other followers of Luther developed them; and the irony, of course, lies in the fact that the new Luther research seriously wonders whether this view differs from Luther's own views. Even those who do not want to set Luther and the Lutheran confessions in tension with each other have to admit that in both the Lutheran and Reformed doctrines of salvation there are differing orientations.

Another kind of assessment of the idea of union and the approach of the Eastern Orthodox view of deification and the Roman Catholic doctrine of justification emerges in the writings of more conciliar Evangelicals. The Baptist Clark Pinnock of Canada is perhaps the ablest and most well-known spokesperson for this view. Pinnock recently expounded his view of the idea of union as the central category of an evangelical theology of salvation in his major pneumatological work, *Flame*

Aghiorgoussis as expressed in his essay "Orthodox Soteriology" in *Salvation in Christ: A Lutheran-Orthodox Dialogue*, J. Meyendorff and R. Tobias, eds. (Minneapolis: Fortress Press, 1992) 48–49.

[61] Fairbairn, op. cit., 46.
[62] Ibid., 47.
[63] Ibid., 50.

of Love: A Theology of the Holy Spirit.[64] That book is unique in that it discusses the main systematic topics, such as Trinity, creation, revelation, Christology, and the church, from an explicitly pneumatological perspective. In other words, he has written a "pneumatological systematic theology," which includes a "pneumatological soteriology." He wants to challenge a theology that in general has given to the Spirit only a secondary role.[65] The appeal of this work and Pinnock's related writings on the Spirit comes from its experiential, almost enthusiastic style. Clearly, this is a sort of "testimony book" that is also a systematic theology.[66] He wants to engage both the mind and the heart, unlike most theologians.

Pinnock's approach to soteriology, the doctrine of salvation, is unique in comparison with most Protestant theologians. It draws heavily from the Eastern pneumatological doctrine of salvation. Not insignificantly, the chapter on salvation in *Flame of Love* is titled "Spirit and Union." He reminds us that when we look at salvation from the standpoint of the Spirit, we view it in relational and affective terms. Rather than focusing on standard Protestant guilt and sin categories, Pinnock searches for a concept of salvation that has its goal in transformation, personal relationship, union. He describes beautifully the image of salvation as the embrace of God, following Bernard of Clairvaux: "If the father kisses the Son and the Son receives the kiss, it is appropriate to think of the Holy Spirit as the kiss."[67]

Although there are various facets to salvation, the goal is glorification and union with God, the Spirit. "We are destined to find our true selves in God, in whom we live and move and have our being. Christ dwells in our hearts by faith, and Spirit sweeps us up into the love of God."[68] The ancient concept that has captured this union dimension is the Eastern doctrine of *theosis*. Insightfully Pinnock notes that if we appreciated the prospect of union with God more, we would not think to complain as much about the arduousness of the journey. At the end of our journey we will be enfolded in trinitarian love through the Spirit.[69]

When the Bible—and Pinnock—comes the closest to describing the overall goal of the Christian life, namely union, it employs sexual im-

[64] Clark Pinnock, *Flame of Love: A Theology of the Holy Spirit* (Downers Grove, Ill.: InterVarsity Press, 1996).
[65] Ibid., 10–11.
[66] Ibid., 12.
[67] Ibid., 150.
[68] Ibid., 150.
[69] Ibid., 151–52.

agery. In Paul's writings, the love of husband and wife points to the mystery of Christ's love for us (Eph 5:31). This intimate imagery links salvation to the fulfillment of our deepest desires as gendered creatures. This joyful celebration of the holy mysteries of Christian faith rings out in the Orthodox liturgy: "Let us rejoice and exult and give him glory, for the marriage of the Lamb has come, and his bride has made herself ready."[70]

Further employing the imagery of love and sexuality, Pinnock says that if salvation is union, conversion is awakening to love. The Spirit is calling the wayward to return to the Father's embrace. On the one hand, the invitation from the Father comes by grace, and he is the initiator. On the other hand, the Spirit may draw, but people must consent. The Spirit helps us, but we are also coworkers with God. We work out our salvation, while God is at work in us (Phil 2:12-13). Conversion requires an interplay of grace and assent.[71]

In a pneumatological soteriology, conversion can also be described as an event of the life-giving Spirit (2 Cor 3:6). "It is living water within, springing up to eternal life (John 4:10, 14; 7:37-39). The risen Lord breathed on the apostles and said, 'Receive the Holy Spirit' (John 20:22). This was reminiscent of God's breathing life into Adam's nostrils and of the breath blowing over the valley of dead bones."[72]

Nor has Pinnock failed to grasp the cosmic orientation of the Eastern soteriology and pneumatology. In his great appreciation of an unlimited ministry of the Spirit, he recognizes there is a "cosmic range to the operations of the Spirit."[73] The emphasis on the Spirit's work in salvation should not be read as a denial of the creative work on which it is based, as too often has been the case.[74] Pinnock argues that by acknowledging the work of the Spirit in creation, we are actually allowed a more universal perspective of the Spirit's ministry where the preparatory work for hearing the gospel is not set in an antithesis with the fulfillment of the gospel in Christ.[75] "What one encounters in Jesus is the fulfillment of previous invitations of the Spirit."[76] In his openness to the

[70] Ibid., 152–53; quote on 153.
[71] Ibid., 157–59.
[72] Ibid., 163.
[73] Ibid., 49.
[74] Ibid., 51. A case in point is the evangelical theologian W. H. Griffith Thomas in *The Holy Spirit of God* (Grand Rapids, Mich.: Eerdmans, 1964) 187, 196, 201, who prefers to bypass the cosmic activities of the Spirit as he sees them threatening the uniqueness of the gospel.
[75] Pinnock, op. cit., 63.
[76] Ibid., 63.

workings of the Spirit in other religions, too, Pinnock argues that access to grace is less of a problem for a *pneumatologically* based theology of religions than for an exclusively christologically anchored one. Whereas the incarnation of the Son was confined to a specific place in time and history, its universal effects, through the ministry of the Spirit, can be transmitted to the farthest ends of the earth.[77]

In the next chapter we will critically analyze the results of major contemporary dialogues, between Lutherans and Orthodox and between Lutherans and Roman Cahtolics, concerning salvation. We will attempt to ascertain ecumenical prospects and challenges. Futhermore, in order to broaden typical ecumenical discourse, we will both highlight the results of the newer dialogue between Roman Catholics and Pentecostals and discuss the potential for Orthodox–Pentecostal dialogue. This discussion of the various dialogues will be limited: only those aspects which highlight and develop the main question of this study, the idea of union as it relates to justification and deification, will be taken up.

[77] Pinnock, *Flame of Love*, 188.

6

Salvation as Union:
Towards an Ecumenical Convergence

1. "Salvation as Justification and Deification" in Lutheran-Orthodox Conversations

The Lutheran and the Orthodox churches are both pioneers of the ecumenical movement; they have also issued a number of official statements concerning the ecumenical commitment and ecumenical work between these two churches.[1] In fact, their bilateral relations go back to the latter part of the sixteenth century to the correspondence between Patriarch Jeremiah II of Constantinople and some Tübingen theologians from 1573 and 1581.[2] Since the end of the 1950s, a number of bilateral Lutheran-Orthodox dialogues have been conducted with a focus on the question of salvation, especially the relationship between deification and justification.

With regard to the issue of deification and its relation to the Lutheran concept of justification by faith, German Lutheran theology has been quite reserved, generally speaking, whereas the Finnish Lutheran Church has pioneered, on the basis and under the leadership of the Mannermaa School, a much more appreciative standpoint. Already in

---

[1] See further, Commission on Faith and Order, *The Orthodox Church and the Churches of the Reformation: A Survey of Orthodox-Protestant Dialogues* (Geneva: World Council of Churches, 1975).

[2] The basic work here is Dorothea Wendebourg, *Reformation und Oikonomia: Der ökumenische Briefwechsel zwischen der Leitung der Württembergischen Kirche und Patriarch Jeremias II. Von Konstantinopel in den Jahren 1573–1581* (Göttingen: Vandenhoeck & Ruprecht, 1986).

the 1970s, the Finnish Lutheran Church, in its conversations with the Russian Orthodox Church, adopted a number of soteriological state-ments which compare the Lutheran doctrine of justification with the Orthodox view of deification/*theosis*.[3] Since the publication of the Finnish-Russian dialogue results in English,[4] other regional conversa-tions have made use of them.[5]

The general Lutheran reservation with regard to the concept of *theo-sis* comes to focus in a comment from the Russian Orthodox dialogue partner to a Finnish theologian:

> I participated in a dialogue with German Lutherans, and there the word "deification" had to be deleted from the text. It was totally incomprehen-sible for the German Lutherans. But in your presentation that word is in place. One and the same Luther, and nevertheless such a big difference between opinions! I do rejoice that the opinion presented in this paper [of Simo Peura] is so close to our own [Orthodox] views.[6]

Recently, American Lutherans have come to appreciate this more conciliar attitude much more than Germans.

The background to the reserved attitude among the majority of Lutheran theologians and ecumenists lies in the fact that for centuries, at least from the time of the Reformation, the Protestant doctrine of jus-tification and the Eastern doctrine of deification have been seen as ex-clusive of and contradictory to each other. For example, both Karl Barth and Albrecht Ritschl regarded deification as an abominable glorifica-tion of man, a sort of *theologia gloriae* (theology of glory), to be con-

[3] For a synopsis in English, see Risto Saarinen, "Salvation in the Lutheran-Orthodox Dialogue: A Comparative Perspective," *Pro Ecclesia* 5 (1996) 202–13. It is noteworthy that even the Evangelical Church of Germany (EKD), which has been the most ardent critic of Eastern soteriology, in the fifth round of conversations with the Romanian Orthodox Church (1988), could produce a joint document *Rechtfertigung und Verherrlichung (Theosis) des Menschen durch Jesus Christus*. EKD-Studienheft 23 (Hermannsburg: Missionsverlag Herrmansburg, 1988). See also Heinz Joachim Held, "Glaube und Liebe in der Erlangung des Heils," in *Das Heil in Christus und die Heilung der Welt*, EKD-Studienhelft 20 (Her-mannsburg: Missionsverlag Herrmansburg, 1985).

[4] Hannu Kamppuri, ed. *Dialogue between Neighbours, The Theological Conversations be-tween the Evangelical-Lutheran Church of Finland and the Russian Orthodox Church 1970–1986* (Helsinki: Luther-Agricola Society, 1986). See also R. Saarinen, "25 Jahre theologische Gespräche zwischen Evangelisch-Lutherischer Kirche Finnlands und Moskauer Patriar-chat," Ökumenische Rundschau 4 (1995).

[5] For a comprehensive analysis of the Lutheran-Orthodox dialogues both at regional and international levels, see Risto Saarinen, *Faith and Holiness: Lutheran-Orthodox Dialogue 1959–1994* (Göttingen: Vandenhoeck & Ruprecht, 1997). My discussion is deeply in-debted to this careful and well-documented study.

[6] Cited in Saarinen, *Faith and Holiness*, 9.

trasted to the Reformation ideal of *theologia crucis,* the theology of the cross. The idea of deification has also been seen as a "false" metaphysics which borders on a "physical" notion of divinization.[7]

Risto Saarinen has posited that the Lutheran theology of salvation could perhaps be labeled a "faith" approach and the Eastern counterpart a "holiness" view. The Lutheran paradigm of faith "stands for trust in things unseen, a trust to God's promise of forgiveness. This view of salvation emphasizes justification by faith alone and speaks of the Christian life as a God-given gift that calls for unselfish love." The Orthodox paradigm of holiness stands for the healing, restorative process in Christians, the way leading to *theosis* or glorification. The paradigm of holiness articulates the process of salvation with the help of "an abundant vocabulary which comprehends both the sacramental life of the church and the individual's striving for perfection. This paradigm further presupposes that a real, although hidden, process of improvement takes place in the life of the Christian."[8]

Rather than trying to summarize in any comprehensive way the numerous regional and global dialogues between the Orthodox and Lutherans, I will focus on the relationship between deification and justification as it was first discussed in the Russian-Finnish dialogue, since that dialogue has been the catalyst for all others. Other dialogues have taken notice of its results and either affirmed or criticized them. In general, it seems that currently most Lutherans are becoming more and more favorable to the emerging convergence between these two traditions as they were first explicated in the Russian-Finnish dialogue. I will then take a briefer look at some other dialogues that have raised legitimate theological questions about the understanding of salvation between these two churches.

In the beginning stages of the Russian-Finnish dialogue there was a sincere effort to find a common foundation and language for the doctrine of salvation. Illustrating this conciliar spirit, the following thesis from 1974 couples the crucial Eastern concept of "participation in divine life" with the Lutheran "faith alone" emphasis: "Whoever truly believes the Gospel and receives the sacraments in faith is given by God a share in the Divine Life. Through faith Christ dwells in his heart (Eph 3:17)."[9] The reason this particular dialogue between the Orthodox and Lutherans

[7] Ibid., 9–10.
[8] Ibid., 242.
[9] Ibid., 36. Saarinen gives detailed source information on the unpublished dialogue— materials which for the most part are not available to the public.

was able to find common ground at such an early stage is that the Lutheran partner defined the Lutheran approach in a way that anchored it firmly in patristic theology. The Lutheran delegation also emphasized the fact that there is no such thing as an undifferentiated "Protestant" theology, but rather there are a variety of Protestant *theologies* (Lutheran, Reformed, Methodist, and so on). Furthermore, the Finnish dialogue team was already influenced by the groundbreaking work of Tuomo Mannermaa and his younger colleagues. Their pronounced aim was to find a common ground between Luther's insistence on Christ present through faith and the Eastern idea of participation in divine life.

The Lutheran biblical scholar Jukka Thuren presented a paper in 1976 titled "Salvation as Justification and Deification." After the discussion of the doctrine of justification in the Bible, Thuren subjected 2 Peter 1:4 to exegetical analysis. He defended the view that in contrast to many contemporary Hellenistic types of deification in Philo, Apollonius of Tyana, Gnostics, and others, 2 Peter expresses an idea *sui generis*. He contended that although the Pauline view of justification in general uses different terminology from 2 Peter, the two are not mutually exclusive. The Pauline view of the Christian as "new creation" corresponds to the Petrine view of "participation in the divine nature."[10]

In light of these developments, it is no wonder that the Finnish-Lutheran dialogue produced a highly influential soteriological document in Kiev 1977 titled "Salvation as Justification and Deification." The preamble to the theses claims that

> Until recently, there has been a predominant opinion that the Lutheran and Orthodox doctrines of salvation greatly differ from each other. In the conversations, however, it has become evident that both these important aspects of salvation discussed in the conversations have a strong New Testament basis and there is great unanimity with regard to them both.[11]

It was found that the doctrine of deification covers the idea of a Christian's life as righteous and sinful at the same time, as Lutheran theology has always emphasized. The idea of deification makes more explicit what is sometimes in danger of being under-emphasized in Lutheranism, namely the sanative role of grace: "When the Christian has been justified, he takes a new road leading to deification."[12]

[10] Ibid., 38–39.
[11] H. Kamppuri, ed., op. cit., 73.
[12] Ibid., 75.

The Russian Orthodox team also made clear already in the early stages of the dialogue in the 1970s that they do not necessarily see *theosis* as opposing Luther's view of salvation. Bishop Mihail argued that Luther's *Lectures on Galatians,* one of the main soteriological works of the Reformer, in which Luther claims that the Christian becomes "one person" with Christ, approaches the Orthodox concept of union. Another Orthodox dialogue member, Vasiliy Stoikov, also stressed the idea that the understanding of grace as participation in divine life may well serve as the common ground for Orthodox and Lutheran theologies.[13]

In a later dialogue paper titled "Salvation of a Christian is in His Deification and Justification," Mihail considerably expanded his conciliar approach. Mihail builds his case on the biblical witness and the church fathers. Surprisingly, he also quotes with approval Augustine and some modern Roman Catholic voices such as Michael Schmaus and Teilhard de Chardin. The Russian bishop freely admits that even though the word "deification" does not occur in the Bible as such, "a prominent idea installed in it is proclaimed on many biblical pages."[14] Not only 2 Peter 1:4, but also many passages in the book of Hebrews that relate to the high priestly work of Christ and to sanctification are referred to in his presentation, as well as a host of Johannine passages. In an ecumenically sensitive way, Mihail then outlines the Orthodox understanding of the doctrine of justification (we have to keep in mind the fact that Orthodox theology seldom if ever even uses the terminology of justification):

> This great gift—justification, making us sons of God, right to come to Him with repentance, that we receive in the Sacrament of Baptism when we are reborn by the water and the Spirit (Jn 3:5), and became a "new creation" (2 Cor 5:17), and we get a possibility to go along the path of growing in holiness, along the way of deification, fighting with sinfulness and despite of it.[15]

Echoing this conciliar spirit, the 1977 common theses placed justification and deification side by side and found in the idea of participation a common ground between Lutheranism and Orthodoxy: "In Holy Baptism we become participants in Christ in a real way. . . . Thus we are justified in Baptism and deification begins, i.e., participation in divine life."[16]

---

[13] Saarinen, *Faith and Holiness,* 39.
[14] Ibid., 41.
[15] Ibid., 42.
[16] Ibid., 44.

Similarly, the fourth thesis of the 1977 session of the Russian-Finnish dialogue was ecumenically groundbreaking in that it was most probably the first time that any Lutheran church ever made an official statement concerning deification:

> When the Christian has been justified, he takes a new road leading to deification. The Church understands it to be a process of growing in holiness or coming closer and closer to God. "But we all, with open face beholding as in a mirror the glory of the Lord, are changed into the same image from glory to glory, even as by the Spirit of the Lord" (2 Cor 3:18). Deification takes place under the influence of the grace of the Holy Spirit by a deep and sincere faith, together with hope and permeated by love" (1 Cor 13:13).[17]

Later on, among Lutherans, a question was raised whether this formulation compromises two tenets dear to Lutheranism, namely the lack of free will in the human being with regard to salvation and the critical role of faith. In response to these concerns, it was noted that what the thesis says is to oppose an absolute "quietism," the view according to which the human person would be like a dead log in the salvation process, and that the role of faith is duly taken into consideration in the formulation "Deification takes place . . . by a deep and sincere faith."

In a remarkable way, while combating the dangers of Pelagianism but approaching the Eastern free will emphasis, the common statement further explained the relationship between the grace of God and human initiative: "Grace never does violence to a man's personal will, but exerts its influence through it and with it. Every one has the possibility to refuse consent to God's will or, by the help of the Holy Spirit, to consent to it."[18] For the Orthodox party, to whom freedom belongs to the ontology of the human being, the accent on the relative freedom of human will is an indispensable theological conviction. For Lutherans, the question of the role of the will in salvation, in my opinion, is an unresolved problem, and consequently, leads to serious intra-Lutheran debates.

Another theological conviction among the Orthodox that has traditionally been felt extremely problematic in Lutheran theology is the question of good deeds in salvation. In his 1980 address to the Russian-Finnish dialogue, "Faith and Love in Salvation," Bishop Mihail reiterated the "classical formula of scholastic Orthodox theology," according to which, "The man is saved by faith and by good deeds." In order to

[17] Ibid., 44.
[18] Ibid., 46.

further a correct understanding of this formula, Mihail made clear that it does not mean separating faith from love; neither does it mean that faith would only be an intellectual attitude nor that salvation in the biblical sense of the word would be received on the basis of human merits. The core in the Orthodox understanding of faith is that faith is "devotedness to God," "trust to God which is interrelated with love to God." Consequently, if faith is "impregnated with love, good deeds are not considered separate from faith, an addition to it, but its fruit, the fruit of living, loving, and therefore, saving faith."[19] Saarinen correctly concludes from these statements that the Orthodox representative clearly approaches the Lutheran understanding of salvation by faith alone. The approaches of the Finnish Lutheran and Russian Orthodox theologians are thus complementary in a very ecumenical manner.[20]

Having summarized the main outcomes of the Russian-Finnish Lutheran-Orthodox dialogue, it is time to briefly compare the results with other regional dialogues and the international dialogue. In light of the fact that German Lutheranism has been so extremely reserved about the Eastern doctrine of salvation, ecumenically it is highly significant that at the end of the 1980s, as result of extensive mutual talks, even the Evangelical Church of Germany (EKD), which has been the most ardent critic of Eastern soteriology, in the fifth round of conversations with the Romanian Orthodox Church (1988), could produce a joint document titled "Justification and Glorification *(Theosis)* of the Human Person in Jesus Christ." Even though its tone is more reserved than that of the Russian-Finnish dialogue's, it takes significant ecumenical steps.[21] An indication of the more cautious approach of this dialogue in comparison to the Russian-Finnish conversations is that terms such as "freedom of the will," "consent," "cooperation," and the like are avoided, and thus the text reads more "Lutheran."[22]

Perhaps the lasting result of the Russian-EKD dialogue is that both parties committed themselves to clearing up long-standing prejudices and misunderstandings. In his extensive paper, the Lutheran Georg Kretschmar outlined similarities between Athanasius and Luther. He freely acknowledged that the traditional Protestant picture of the "physical doctrine of redemption" in Orthodox soteriology is only to some extent adequate. When the Orthodox speak of the deification of human

[19] Ibid., 51.
[20] Ibid., 51.
[21] Cf. German references in note 3 above.
[22] Saarinen, *Faith and Holiness*, 102.

beings, they certainly mean much more than just a change in morals and thoughts. Kretschmar further claimed that Luther did indeed receive some central soteriological thoughts from the Greek fathers. Luther could speak of the "likeness" of the Christian to Christ; Luther also occasionally used the Athanasian rule according to which God became human in order that the human person might become God. What is important to Lutherans is that the doctrine of deification does not mean the same as a theology of glory. The reason is that when the Christian becomes Christlike, he is not only glorified but also at the same time crucified with Christ. The likeness leads not only to the glory, but also to the cross; this is the result of an "alien" work of God. Saarinen summarizes the significance of Kretschmar's dialogue input:

> Kretschmar thus undertakes a revision of the traditional Protestant view. According to that view, the Orthodox doctrine of deification as a physical-materialistic transformation is an expression of anthropocentric *theologia gloriae* and consequently incompatible with true Protestantism which stresses ethics and spirit as opposed to the naturalistic categories of thought.[23]

Significantly enough, Bishop Mihail also emphasizes the value of Luther's theology of the cross for Orthodox soteriology. According to the Orthodox bishop, the theology of the cross is "equivalent to the view of the holy Fathers."[24]

After all this ecumenical convergence, the following paragraph from the 1992 dialogue paper by the Lutheran Simo Peura, who has written a major study on the motif of deification in Luther, does not seem as "non-Lutheran" as one might expect in light of the historical controversies between Lutheranism and Orthodoxy. It summarizes and elaborates much of the previous work and builds on the results of the new paradigm in Lutheran studies:

> This life of the Christian in Christ is called in the Lutheran tradition participation in God, although it is often expressed in different terms. The sacramental word and sacraments and faith firstly bring it about that Christ joins himself in a real, but hidden way to the sinner. Participation in Christ and the divine nature means then that in the sinner there takes place a profound and fundamental renewal. From this wells forth true love of God and one's neighbour. In Lutheranism, this is called by the name, new birth, justification, adoption by God, deification of man.[25]

[23] Ibid., 104.
[24] Ibid.
[25] Ibid., 74.

The dialogue between the EKD and the Romanian Orthodox Church deserves special attention as well since it could build upon earlier conversations on the topic of salvation; the years 1985–1991 were titled, "Justification, Theosis, Synergeia." The fourth session was titled "Salvation in Christ and Healing of the World." The latter part of the title, as one would assume in light of recent ecumenical developments, does not refer to social ethics but to the traditional Orthodox doctrine of salvation as encompassing cosmic dimensions. The Orthodox Dimitru Radu emphasizes what he calls the "ontological aspect" of the work of Christ, which includes liberation from suffering and death and the filling of human nature with divinity. What salvation is all about is basically a broadening of the divine penetration of Christ to all human nature. From that perspective, the incarnation of Christ already implies the renewal of all humanity, even all creation. According to Radu, Jesus Christ became gradually permeated by the Holy Spirit and, consequently, by the divine nature; this very same principle applies to the salvation of human beings in general. "The whole human nature of Christians, their souls and bodies, is renewed and deified and they unite with God through the work of the Holy Spirit. This is a process of 'ontological restitution and growth.'" He also argues that Luther's view, according to which the Holy Spirit begins his work already in this life, converges with the Orthodox doctrine.[26]

The EKD theologian Heinz Joachim Held takes his point of departure from the Orthodox soteriology and the ecumenical developments of the Russian-Finnish dialogue, in his paper titled "Faith and Love as Constituents of Salvation." As is well known, Lutherans typically talk about faith as the key to salvation, whereas for the Orthodox, faith without love is a "dead" faith. Held comes to the conclusion that traces of the idea of deification can be found within Protestantism. With regard to the question of the relationship between justification and sanctification, he responds that justification means renewal of the heart. In other words, Held encourages Protestants to see sanctification as a necessary part of justification and as a reality in which some synergy must be presupposed.[27]

To highlight the ecumenical significance of these perspectives, one need only take note of the much more traditional stance taken by the Lutheran side in the American Lutheran-Orthodox dialogue which

[26] Ibid., 148–49; quote 149; the text in quotation is Saarinen's paraphrase of Radu's argumentation.
[27] Ibid., 148–49.

radically distinguishes between justification and sanctification both conceptually and sequentially: "For the Lutherans, 'justification' and 'sanctification' are two distinct theological categories, one designating God's declaration of righteousness, the other the gradual process of growth in the Christian life."[28] That standpoint is a legitimate interpretation in Lutheranism, it goes back, as was noticed earlier, to the confessional statements. But ecumenically, it sets Lutheranism in opposition to both Orthodox and Catholic theologies as well as to Luther's own theology. The American dialogue's title to the common statement, "Christ 'In Us' and Christ 'For Us,'" reflecting Orthodox and Lutheran approaches to salvation respectively, makes the same kind of distinction.

Although the EKD did not choose to use the terminology of deification, the way they defined the doctrine of justification approaches the views of the Orthodox and Roman Catholic Churches: "In justification the faithful person receives the gift of reconciliation and renewal in Christ for himself (subjectively) as new life. Through faith which is manifest in good works he really (actualiter) participates in this reconciliation and becomes a new creation. The gift of renewal and reconciliation bears fruit and is manifest in love, in all human relationships, in the vertical relation towards God, in the horizontal relations towards the neighbor."[29] Commensurably, the Romanian Orthodox counterpart also expressed a conciliar attitude in making a distinction between two senses of deification. *Theosis* in a wider sense begins in baptism and continues throughout the Christian's life; "it is an ontological restitution of the human nature." Deification in its narrower sense means the eschatological consummation of the process which leads the Christian "over the limits of his nature and powers to the supernatural level of God." In other words, the two senses of deification and justification are thus a continuum. Saarinen notes that this distinction between the two stages is helpful because the first does not imply any such superhuman transformation, of which all Protestants are skeptical.[30]

Before summing up the results of the Orthodox-Lutheran conversations, a note, especially important to Orthodox theology, is in order, namely, the role of the Holy Spirit in salvation. Orthodox theology in

---

[28] "Christ 'In Us' and Christ 'For Us' in Lutheran and Orthodox Theology: Common Statement of the Lutheran Orthodox Dialogue in America," in John Meyendorff and Robert Tobias, eds., *Salvation in Christ: A Lutheran-Orthodox Dialogue* (Minneapolis: Augsburg, 1992) 19.

[29] Saarinen, *Faith and Holiness*, 149.

[30] Ibid., 151.

general and soteriology in particular is heavily imbued by pneumatological orientations. Understandably, deification is a pneumatologically
loaded image of salvation; this was aptly noticed in the Russian-Finnish
dialogue as well. Defining "the new road leading to deification" as a
"process of growing in holiness," the joint document cites two important Pauline texts: "But we all, with open face beholding as in a mirror
the glory of the Lord, are changed into the same image from glory to
glory, even as by the Spirit of the Lord" (2 Cor 3:18). Deification takes
place under the influence of the grace of the Holy Spirit by a deep and
sincere faith, together with hope and permeated by love (1 Cor 13:13).[31]
Ecumenically, it is helpful to notice that in Luther's own theology, especially as it has been explicated in the new interpretation, pneumatological perspectives have emerged in a more visible way. The leading
idea, Christ present through faith, can also be expressed pneumatically:
it is through the Spirit of Christ—it has to be remembered that Luther
always thinks Christologically—that mediation of salvatory gifts is accomplished. Participation in God is possible only through the Spirit of
Christ, the Spirit of adoption.[32]

The main ecumenical results and challenges of Orthodox-Lutheran
relationships with regard to the doctrine of salvation may be summarized as follows:

First, there is an emerging consensus that the Orthodox idea of the
believer's union with God, *theosis*, regardless of differing language, can
be compatible with the Western notion of participation in God, an idea
that is an essential part of the doctrine of justification by faith.

Second, there are two dominant approaches to the doctrine of justification in Protestant theology in general and in Lutheranism in particular. Luther's own theology of salvation, in contrast to the theologies
of the Lutheran confessions, comes much closer to the idea of union.
The official confessional standpoint of Lutheranism sets the doctrine of
justification in antithesis to the Orthodox idea of union. It is a theological and ecumenical decision to follow one or the other of these theologies;
it also touches deeply the question of identity within Lutheranism—
whether to build it on Luther's own theology or the subsequent confessional statements as developed by Philip Melanchthon and other
followers of Luther.

---

[31] H. Kamppuri, ed., *Dialogue Between Neighbours*, 75.
[32] For a brief summary of the idea of adoption in Luther, see Risto Saarinen, "The
Presence of God in Luther's Theology," *Lutheran Quarterly* 3:1 (1994) 9–10.

Third, it has become evident that the idea of union is a leading theme both in the Orthodox notion of deification and in that form of the Lutheran doctrine of justification that regards the living presence of Christ in the believer as justification.

Fourth, the thorny question of the relationship between justification and sanctification consequently comes to new light as a result of this convergence. Whereas the school theology of Protestantism, including the confessional approach of Lutheranism, has made a definite distinction between these two, for Orthodox theology as well as Luther's own theology, such a distinction is foreign. Deification and justification mean the change of the believer (sanctification), not only the change of her status (the forensic aspect of justification).

Fifth, the role of the Holy Spirit has also come to a new light in Protestant theology, especially in its Lutheran form, as a result of the discovery of the idea of the presence of Christ as justification. Whereas the doctrine of salvation in typical Protestant theologies has tended to be dominated by christological orientations, this new search of Protestant soteriology elevates the role of the Spirit to the place the Spirit has always occupied in Eastern theology: the works of Christ and the Spirit are mutually conditioned, and the salvatory work of Christ is communicated to the believer only through the work of the Spirit. Deification and justification is a spirited work of the triune God.

Sixth, the Orthodox doctrine of salvation has the potential of connecting soteriology with the doctrines of creation and anthropology in more comprehensive terms than Western theology has done. The cosmic orientation of Eastern patristic theology, as developed in the later Eastern theologies, with a view to the transformation of the whole cosmos into life eternal under one God, in union with God, opens unprecedented perspectives on the question of continuity versus discontinuity in the work of the triune God. The implications for the doctrine of creation, earth-keeping, or similar concerns are yet to be spelled out; even Eastern theology has not made this connection explicit. Interestingly enough, Jürgen Moltmann in his Christology has taken a lead from this cosmic orientation of Eastern patristic theology and offered a helpful critique of the Western Enlightenment narrowing of Christology; though even Moltmann has not elaborated on the soteriological implications.[33]

---

[33] See further, Jürgen Moltmann, *The Way of Jesus Christ: Christology in Messianic Dimension*, Margaret Kohl, trans. (Minneapolis: Fortress Press, 1993).

2. Justification and Sanctification in the
Roman Catholic-Lutheran Conversations

> The doctrine of justification was of central importance for the Lutheran
> Reformation of the sixteenth century. It was held to be the "first and chief
> article"[34] and at the same time the "ruler and judge over all other Christian
> Doctrines."[35] The doctrine of justification was particularly asserted and de-
> fended in its Reformation shape and special valuation over against the
> Roman Catholic Church and theology of that time, which in turn asserted
> and defended a doctrine of justification with a different character. From the
> Reformation perspective, justification was the crux of all the disputes. Doc-
> trinal condemnations were put forward both in the Lutheran confessions
> and by the Roman Catholic Church's Council of Trent. These condemna-
> tions are still valid today and thus have a church-dividing effect.[36]

Thus begins the Preamble to the *Joint Declaration on the Doctrine of Justification* which on October 31, 1999, was signed by the Roman Catholic Church and the member churches of the Lutheran World Federation which represents over 62 million of the world's more than 65 million Lutherans, non-ecumenical bodies such as the Lutheran Church— Missouri Synod not being members. This agreement, the product of decades of dialogue that started at the close of the Second Vatican Council, lifted the sixteenth-century church-dividing condemnations concerning the doctrine of justification. Several key statements and studies preceded the 1999 signing: *Justification by Faith* (1983),[37] *The Condemnations of the Reformation Era—Do They Still Divide?* (1988), and *Justification by Faith: Do the Sixteenth-Century Condemnations Still Apply?* (1989) and *Church and Justification* (1994)[38] among others.[39]

[34] The Smalcald Articles, II, 1; in *The Book of Concord: The Confessions of the Evangelical Lutheran Church*, Robert Kolb and Timothy J. Wengert, eds. (Minneapolis: Fortress Press, 2000) 292 (hereafter BD).

[35] *WA* 39, I, 205.

[36] The Lutheran World Federation and the Roman Catholic Church, *Joint Declaration on the Doctrine of Justification*, Preamble (Grand Rapids, Mich.: Eerdmans, 2000) 9.

[37] H. George Anderson, T. Austin Murphy, and Joseph A. Burgess, eds., *Justification by Faith*, Lutherans and Catholics in Dialogue VII (Minneapolis: Augsburg Publishing House, 1985).

[38] Karl Lehmann and Wolfhart Pannenberg, eds., *The Condemnations of the Reformation Era: Do They Still Divide?* Margaret Kohl, trans. (Minneapolis: Fortress Press, 1990), Karl Lehmann, Michael Root, and William G. Rusch, eds., *Justification by Faith: Do the Sixteenth-Century Condemnations Still Apply?* (New York: Continuum 1997), Lutheran-Roman Catholic Joint Commission, *Church and Justification* (Geneva: Lutheran World Federation, 1994).

[39] See further, William G. Rusch, ed., *Justification and the Future of the Ecumenical Movement: The Joint Declaration on the Doctrine of Justification*, Unitas Books (Collegeville: Liturgical Press, 2003).

What does this agreement mean ecumenically and theologically? Several things have to be taken into account to place it in a proper perspective. First, this is not a comprehensive ecumenical agreement between these two churches in terms of Lutherans and Roman Catholics joining together. Extremely important and critical issues, such as the papacy, still divide Lutherans and Catholics. Second, this is not even a comprehensive agreement on salvation, rather

> [the] Joint Declaration has this intention: namely, to show that on the basis of their dialogue the subscribing Lutheran churches and the Roman Catholic Church are now able to articulate a common understanding of our justification by God's grace through faith in Christ. It does not cover all that either church teaches about justification; it does encompass a consensus on basic truths of the doctrine of justification and shows that the remaining differences in its explication are no longer the occasion for doctrinal condemnations (paragraph #5).

The structure of the document itself reveals its approach. On each major topic, there is first a common statement followed by qualifications and specifications by both parties. Third, consequently, this agreement does not mean overlooking or forgetting earlier painful divisions. There is an honest desire to go beyond the Reformation/Counter-Reformation mutual condemnations, but they can never be undone: "in overcoming the earlier controversial questions and doctrinal condemnations, the churches neither take the condemnations lightly nor do they disavow their own past. On the contrary, this Declaration is shaped by the conviction that in their respective histories our churches have come to new insights" (#7).

Before going on to a more detailed treatment of the Joint Declaration, a brief look at the classical Catholic and Lutheran formulations of the doctrine of justification will be offered; this is the background against which there arose the need to engage in these decades-long dialogues.

The only time the Roman Catholic Church has definitively defined its doctrine of justification was at the Council of Trent; in its sixth session on January 13, 1547, as a response to the Reformation, the main outline of the Catholic view was defined. It has to be noted, however, that even this definition is not a comprehensive doctrine of grace, nor was it meant to be. Its main purpose was to combat the challenges of the Reformers. As in any ecumenical council, at Trent there were several definitive voices and even conflicting interpretations; the decree on justification is a result of those differing orientations. Also, it has to be

remembered that since the Council of Trent the Roman Church has never
attempted any kind of precise formulation of the doctrine of salvation,
not even at Vatican I at the end of the nineteenth century nor at Vatican
II in the 1960s. Therefore, the formulations of Trent are still definitive
for Catholic theology, even if the approach to the doctrine of justification has understandably moved from the medieval "mechanistic" understanding to a more dynamic and personalistic approach in modern times.

The Council declared that because of sin the human being is not
able to bring about justification, nor is the law able to do so.[40] Even
though the human person is not able to turn to God without the pre-
ceding grace in Christ, free assent and human cooperation with the grace
of God is required (#5). The proper way to prepare for the reception of
grace is faith, which means to "believe to be true what has been divinely
revealed and promised," namely, that God justifies the wicked (#6).
Justification is "a transition from the state in which a person is born as
a child of the first Adam to the state of grace and of adoption as children of God" through Jesus Christ; this transition, however, cannot take
place without baptism or at least the desire for it (#4).

Justification is "not only the forgiveness of sins but also . . . the
sanctification and renewal of the inward being by a willing acceptance
of the grace and gifts whereby someone from being unjust becomes just"
(#7). In other words, here the council wants to say that justification is
not only forensic declaration of righteousness before God but consists
of a real change in the believer. Utilizing medieval scholastic language,
the council then introduced the various "causes" of justification: the
final cause is the glory of God, the efficient cause the mercy of God, the
meritorious cause is Christ, and the instrumental cause baptism (#7).

As a result of justification, the believer receives the love of God
that is poured out in the heart by the Holy Spirit and with it the "infused graces" of faith, hope, and charity (#7). Faith is the first stage of
salvation, the foundation and root of all justification, even though faith
does not merit justification (#8). But even the person who has this justifying grace is never in the place of presuming one's salvation (#9) or
predestination (#12), even though God's faithfulness is never to be
doubted nor the gift of perseverance, which is a result of this (#13). Since
justification means a real change in the believer, it may increase as a

---

[40] "Decree on Justification," Council of Trent, Session 6, ch. 1 (in *Decrees of the Ecumenical Councils*, vol. II: *Trent-Vatican II*, Norman P. Tanner, ed. [London: Sheed & Ward/
Washington, D.C.: Georgetown University Press, 1990]). In the following, the "#" in the
main text refers to chapters of session 6.

result of Christian growth (#10); therefore, good deeds are not indifferent to salvation for God does not command the impossible. "Faith alone" in the sense of being complacent about God's commandments is not "saving faith" (#11). Eternal life is to be granted to the justified at the last judgment because of God's grace and as a "reward . . . to be faithfully rendered to their good works and merits" (#16). Justification may also be lost through either loss of faith or the commission of other mortal sins; restoration is possible through the sacrament of penance (#14, 15).

The Lutheran confessions treat the topic of justification in several places, the most important being the Augsburg Confession (1530; especially articles IV, VI, and XX), the Apology of the Augsburg Confession (1531), The Smalcald Articles (1537), and the later Formula of Concord (1577). The foundational passage is Article IV of the Augsburg Confession, "Concerning Justification":

> Likewise, they [the Lutherans] teach that human beings cannot be justified before God by their own powers, merits, or works. But they are justified as a gift on account of Christ through faith when they believe that they are received into grace and that their sins are forgiven on account of Christ, who by his death made satisfaction for our sins. God reckons this faith as righteousness. (Rom 3[:21-26] and 4[:5])

Several things said here define the Lutheran confessional understanding of salvation.[41] First, this is justification before God *(coram Deo)* and not before other human beings *(coram hominibus)*. According to the Lutheran doctrine, while the human being is totally unable to justify herself in relation to God, she has a relative capability to live justly in the society. Second, it is affirmed here that the concept of merit does not belong to the human-God relationship; it is a matter of gift. Third, the cause for justification is Christ *(proper Christum:* because of Christ's merit), and the way to receive it is faith. Justification is based on God's reckoning of Christ's righteousness on our behalf.

Whereas in the Trent document "faith" means primarily intellectual assent, an act of intellect moved by God to embrace the truth of the Gospel, for Lutherans this kind of faith is mere "historical" faith *(fides historica)*. Consequently, in the Catholic doctrine faith is merely the necessary condition and beginning of justification; what justification is substantially is the internal change of the human being; we "are not

[41] I am indebted to Tuomo Mannermaa, *Kristillisen opin vaiheet: Dogmihistorian peruskurssi* (Helsinki: Gaudeamus, 1975) 187.

merely considered to be just but we are truly named and are just, each one of us receiving individually his own justness according to the measure which the Holy Spirit apportions to each one as he wills."[42] The crucial justifying effect is the gift *(donum)* of grace given to the human person, the love of God that becomes an ontological quality. When the Lutherans say that the human being is justified freely by faith because of Christ, the Catholics say that we are justified by faith which works through love poured into our hearts through the Spirit.[43] Consequently, in Catholic theology the concept of "merit" plays a role in the human-God relationship even though it is not on the basis of human merit that salvation is brought about. In their judgment, the Reformation doctrine leads to a "cheap grace."

The Lutheran counter-argument is, of course, that by introducing the category of "merit" in the doctrine of salvation and insisting that we are not saved "by faith alone," the gospel is being transformed into "law." This is actually what Melanchthon says in the Apology of the Augsburg Confession (IV, 7–8). Furthermore, the Apology emphasizes the fact that "justification takes place through a free promise" and therefore, "it follows that we cannot justify ourselves" (Apology IV, 43–44). The law is not the way to salvation; trusting faith in God's promises is. The law is there to condemn us (Apology IV, 38). For Lutherans, trusting faith is much more than "knowledge of history," it is rather "assent to the promise of God" and it means to "desire and to receive the offered promise of the forgiveness of sins and justification." Faith is, furthermore, "that worship which receives the benefits that God offers" (Apology IV, 48–49).

Finally, for the Lutheran confessions, justification is not a process but a completed action before God, even though there is the process of sanctification subsequent to justification. For Catholic theology, justification is a process, and there is no theological distinction between justifying and sanctifying grace, even if sanctification for them is also a process.

Having surveyed briefly the historical definitions of the Catholic and Lutheran doctrines of justification as the background and context of the recent Catholic-Lutheran Joint Declaration on Justification, it is time to analyze that declaration in greater depth. No comprehensive analysis is attempted here. The focal point is the main question of our study: How does this joint declaration highlight the idea of union in the

---

[42] "Decree on Justification," Council of Trent, Session 6, ch. 7.
[43] Mannermaa, *Kristillisen opin vaiheet,* 189.

recent Lutheran and Catholic soteriologies? Are there any fresh ways to
approach the age-old dilemma between the Lutheran confessions' view of
forensic justification and Trent's view of justification as an internal change?
Finally, we ask how all of this relates to the Eastern doctrine of union.

The starting point for the common declaration is the common reading of the Bible: "Our common way of listening to the word of God in
Scripture has led to . . . new insights" (#8; see also #14).[44] In line with
the new developments in biblical studies, it is acknowledged that in the
New Testament there is diversity of meanings attached to the terms
righteousness and *justification;* for example, various Evangelists appropriate the terminology for their own specific contexts (#9). The mani-
fold biblical witness to the doctrine of justification is encapsulated
succinctly in the following summary:

> Justification is the forgiveness of sins (cf. Rom 3:23-25; Acts 13:39; Lk 18:14),
> liberation from the dominating power of sin and death (Rom 5:12-21)
> and from the curse of the law (Gal 3:10–14). It is acceptance into com-
> munion with God—already now, but then fully in God's coming king-
> dom (Rom 5:1f). It unites with Christ and with his death and resurrection
> (Rom 6:5). It occurs in the reception of the Holy Spirit in baptism and in-
> corporation into the one body (Rom 8:1f, 9f; I Cor 12:12f). All this is from
> God alone, for Christ's sake, by grace, through faith in "the gospel of
> God's Son" (Rom 1:1-3). (#11)

What is noteworthy here is an acknowledgment of the fact that
justification not only means forgiveness of sins but also "communion
with God" and union with Christ. On the basis of these biblical delin-
eations and insights from recent ecumenical developments, a remarkable common statement is put forth between Catholics and Lutherans:
"Justification thus means that Christ himself is our righteousness, in
which we share through the Holy Spirit in accord with the will of the
Father" (#15). The affirmation that Christ is our justification forms a
common bridge between two opposing orientations, namely, the
Lutheran confessions' forensic definition and the Catholics' effective
view of justification. This is in fact mentioned directly in the subtitle
4.2. "Justification as Forgiveness of Sins and Making Righteous," the
issue that has historically been the main point of contention:

> . . . God forgives sin by grace and at the same time frees human beings
> from sin's enslaving power and imparts the gift of new life in Christ.

[44] In the following, "#" refers to paragraphs in the Lutheran-Catholic *Joint Declaration on the Doctrine of Justification.*

When persons come by faith to share in Christ, God no longer imputes to them their sin and through the Holy Spirit effects in them an active love. These two aspects of God's gracious action are not to be separated, for persons are by faith united with Christ, who in his person is our righteousness (1 Cor 1:30): both the forgiveness of sin and the saving presence of God himself (#22).

Clearly, the Lutheran partner has taken a significant ecumenical step in mutually agreeing that justification is not only forgiveness of sins but also internal change, even effecting love through the Spirit. The focal point is the union with Christ. The Lutheran qualification to this clause underlines the fact that it is only by virtue of "union with Christ" that one's life is renewed, even though for Lutherans this life-renewing effect is not necessary for justification (#23). Having agreed about this common affirmation, both parties wanted to add some more explanations on this crucial topic. Lutherans say that in the doctrine of "'justification by faith,' a distinction but not a separation is made between justification itself and the renewal of one's way of life that necessarily follows from justification and without which faith does not exist" (#26).

This is a very carefully drafted explanation that also shows the real struggle the Lutheran confessions bring to the question of forgiveness and renewal. This statement attempts to steer a middle course between the one-sided forensic view and the sanative view of Luther himself. The continuation of the Lutheran comment is interesting in that it dares to use the Catholic language of "impartation" of God's love: "Thereby the basis is indicated from which the renewal of life proceeds, for it comes forth from the love of God imparted to the person in justification" (#26). The Catholic counterpart statement reiterates the standard Catholic position according to which justifying grace is always sanative, effective grace, or it is no real justification at all (#27).

Union language is quite evident in the joint declaration. For example, it says, "We confess together that in baptism the Holy Spirit unites one with Christ, justifies, and truly renews the person" (#28). This is an ecumenical consensus that all major Christian traditions would be willing to sign.

Roman Catholics confess with Lutherans that even while justified, Christians are still sinners in need of constant renewal (#28). This is the core of the Lutheran insistence on *simul iustus et peccator* ("just and sinner simultaneously"). Lutherans also believe that even though sin in the justified person is "real sin," it is sin "ruled" by Christ and does not bring about separation from God (#29). Catholics for their part talk about "concupiscence," an inclination to sin that is not counted as a "real sin," since the personal element (which in Catholic theology makes sin sin) is lacking. Only if the person voluntarily separates herself from God does separation happen (#30). It has been one of the disputes in the past to argue whether concupiscence is sin (Lutherans have tended to say *yes*) or not (the Catholic insistence).

In several places the joint declaration talks about human cooperation, which has been another major point of contention. It was mutually agreed that salvation comes "by grace alone" (e.g., #19). "By grace alone" means that human beings are unable to save themselves because of sin (#19). However, it is important for Catholics to underline the role of human "cooperation" in the preparation for and acceptance of justification. Even Lutherans are ready to acknowledge that persons may reject the offer of grace (#20, 21). When it comes to the role of good works, here also some significant ecumenical steps have been taken:

> We confess together that good works—a Christian life lived in faith, hope and love—follow justification and are its fruits. When the justified live in Christ and act in the grace they receive, they bring forth, in biblical terms, good fruit. Since Christians struggle against sin their entire lives, this consequence of justification is also for them an obligation they must fulfill. Thus both Jesus and the apostolic Scriptures admonish Christians to bring forth the works of love (#37).

The confessional difference lies in defining the relation of good works to justification. In the Catholic tradition, good works contribute to growth in grace (#38), while for Lutherans it is important also to emphasize the non-meritorious nature of salvation and the completeness of justification (#39).

The emphasis on the role of the Holy Spirit in justification in several common affirmations provides a helpful reminder of the pneumatological undergirding of salvation: "By grace alone, in faith in Christ's saving work and not because of any merit on our part, we are accepted by God and receive the Holy Spirit, who renews our hearts while equipping and calling us to good works" (#15). In addition, "By the action of the Holy Spirit in baptism, they are granted the gift of salvation" (#25). Many more similar references could be added that highlight the role of the Spirit in salvation.

Now, what are the results and accomplishments of this ecumenical declaration? I will divide my reflections into two themes: the soteriological results and the results addressing wider ecumenical concerns:

The Joint Declaration reveals the emergence of a significant ecumenical consensus on the doctrine of salvation. The main features can be listed as follows:

1. Common Bible reading has helped these Christian traditions to come to appreciate the necessary plurality of the biblical terminology for justification; this in itself suggests that whatever "critical" function the doctrine of justification may serve for the rest of theology, at its best it is qualified and limited.

2. Both churches agree that salvation comes totally by the grace of God through the meritorious work of Christ.

3. Catholics as well as Lutherans agree, though with differing emphases, that human cooperation is called forth to make justification happen in the human person. God does not save anybody against her will, let alone sanctify her.

4. Christ in his person is the human being's justification and righteousness.

5. Justification means both forgiveness of sins (forensic justification; favor) and inner renewal and change. In other words, justification and sanctification form one theological entity.

6. Justification is union with Christ.

7. Justification is the work of the triune God. In contrast to a merely christological orientation to the question of salvation, this dialogue succeeded in highlighting the role of the Spirit in a due manner.

8. The justified person faces the real challenge of sin and vulnerability to turn away from God.

The Joint Declaration challenges both Christian traditions to continue working not only in relation to the other tradition but also within their own theological tradition. For Lutherans, the open questions are the theological relationship between justification and sanctification, the role of human will and freedom, and the role of the Holy Spirit. For Catholics, the real challenges are the nature of sin after justification and the notion of merit.

In terms of wider ecumenical perspectives, it is significant that two theological traditions may agree on the outline of a major doctrine and still retain their differing emphases. First, both Catholics and Lutherans have had to reevaluate their doctrines in order to reach this agreement, but still they did not have to deny the distinctive features of each one's theological and spiritual heritage. Second, the Catholic-Lutheran dialogue shows that with the change of times, and consequent intellectual and theological shifts, new avenues may be taken to overcome the impasse of ancient dividing formulations. Rather than denying the seriousness of hundreds-of-years-old doctrinal definitions, the ecumenical dialogue succeeded in expressing them in a way that was mutually more acceptable. Third, the principle of complementarity is evidenced in this dialogue on salvation. In order to agree on the basic convictions with regard to salvation, different traditions need not try to deny all the differences. Something like the Catholic principle of the "hierarchy of truths" sanctioned at Vatican II (according to which all Catholics have to adhere to certain foundational doctrines to be Catholics, but may still have differing opinions with regard to other Christian doctrines) may be applicable to ecumenical work like this. If so, the existence of various approaches to the doctrine of salvation among Christian churches need not be a threat to conciliarity; it may rather enrich the Christian witness in the world.

Fourth, not only are there differences between various Christian traditions; surprisingly radical differences are to be found amidst any single Christian tradition, not only within Catholicism, which has been so masterful in retaining the unity of the church even though it includes a host of different spiritual and theological movements. Lutherans have had to face the painful challenge of trying to find Lutheran identity vis-à-vis the Catholic church. This has meant a helpful self-scrutiny and return to sources. This ecumenical dialogue did not solve the problem of Lutheran identity, but it kept the question alive. With regard to Lutheranism, the key question is whether the confessions or Luther's own theology serves as *the* definitive statement of what Lutheranism is. The same question emerged, of course, also in the dialogue with the Orthodox church.

3. "Beyond Salvation": Christian Transformation in the Orthodox-Pentecostal Perspective

Over the years it has become my growing belief that it is not mere accident that Pentecostalism and Eastern Orthodoxy—when each mirrors its authentic identity—share very mystical and vibrant characteristics.

> Though the two are dramatically different in many ways (culture, ecclesiology, styles of worship, and missiological strategies, to name a few), they share several beliefs which historically have facilitated a dynamic and often inexpressible Christian experience . . . perhaps most importantly, both maintain that salvation, in its fullest biblical sense, involves communion with God: to be a Christian is far more than having one's legal slate in heaven wiped clean.[45]

This is the opening thesis of the Pentecostal scholar Edmund J. Rybarczyk in his ecumenically groundbreaking study, "Beyond Salvation: An Analysis of the Doctrine of Christian Transformation Comparing Eastern Orthodoxy with Classical Pentecostalism." Rybarczyk freely admits there are many prejudices and misunderstandings between these two churches; some of these conflicts have become more intense with the opening up of Eastern Europe to missionary work from non-Orthodox groups. Still he finds surprisingly many common features between the oldest Christian tradition and one of the newest, such as (1) the fact that both churches are organically structured rather than "top heavy"; (2) the importance of the role of the laity; (3) the primacy of pneumatology in theology and spirituality; (4) a conservative outlook in general; (5) similarities in worldview; (6) emphasis on experience rather than on theology per se; (7) and the ad hoc nature of theology.[46] On top of all these similarities, Rybarczyk argues that the common denominator between Eastern spirituality and Pentecostalism is the mystical nature of both traditions, although Pentecostal theology and spirituality is "only occasionally mystical." To call Eastern Orthodoxy mystical sounds self-evident, but not so for Pentecostalism. As Rybarczyk notes, a recent historical-critical survey of mysticism even fails to mention Pentecostals among the ranks of the mystical.[47] But indeed, typical Pentecostal spirituality and worship include several mystical elements:

> in public meetings they ecstatically speak and sing aloud in unknown tongues, they fall backwards in trance-like states, they sit or stand or kneel stone-silent for extended periods, they pray aloud together in cacophonous ways, they exuberantly shout to God and one another, they believe that praying in an unknown tongue accomplishes untold things in the

---

[45] Edmund J. Rybarczyk, *Beyond Salvation: An Analysis of the Doctrine of Christian Transformation Comparing Eastern Orthodoxy with Classical Pentecostalism*, Ph.D. dissertation, Fuller Theological Seminary, 1999, ii.

[46] Ibid., 5–8.

[47] Denise Lardner Carmody and John Tully Carmody, *Mysticism* (New York: Oxford University Press, 1996).

realm of the invisible, and—to take their grand doctrinal distinctive as an example—they encourage an encounter with God that leaves one's entire being both suffused and sated with the divine presence. . . . In all of these ways they are mystical.[48]

Since both Orthodoxy and Pentecostalism share this mystical and experiential nature, Rybarczyk thinks that both emphasize that to be a Christian is to experience Christ and his Holy Spirit, not only at conversion, but throughout one's Christian life, "in the deepest recesses of one's being." To be saved is far more than receiving forgiveness or having one's relationship to God settled; there is desire for a real transformation of the life of the Christian. Consequently, both Christian families emphasize that it is within the "mystical human core that the Spirit of Christ seeks to have communion with human persons and thereby transform them into His image."[49]

The Orthodox and Pentecostals certainly employ different terminology in their descriptions of salvation. Orthodox theology's favorite term is *theosis*, while Pentecostals usually refer to the highest goal of Christian life as sanctification. For Pentecostals, who are usually theologically less sophisticated than other Western traditions, theology is both of an ad hoc nature and practical. Rarely have they accurately defined terms such as justification and sanctification, and whenever they do they usually follow the standard Western formulations. Their difference from the Protestant school theology is, however, that with the Radical Reformation, Pietism, and Wesleyanism and Holiness Movements, the moment of conversion and subsequent justification is only the first, even though critical, step in the process of transformation, in their terminology, sanctification.

> That is, whereas the believer is cleansed and forgiven at conversion, the life *in Christ*—something expressed by Pentecostals as the life *in Christ's Spirit*—involves far more. Indeed, as they express it, the Christian who is satisfied with conversion alone will likely lead a muted and listless Christian life. Yes, one is indeed cleansed and consecrated at conversion, but one must both also live a life in keeping with that initial moment in one's own salvation history and subsequently allow the Holy Spirit to transform oneself in the depths of one's being.

In all of this, "like their Orthodox counterparts, the Pentecostals believe the Christian walk is comprised of far more than repentance

---

[48] Rybarczyk, op. cit., 3.
[49] Ibid., 11.

and faith."[50] Like the Orthodox, Wesley and Pentecostals are deeply concerned with what happens in the Christian and not just what happens for the Christian.

David Bundy has recently argued that there is a theological and historical convergence between the spirituality of William J. Seymour, the Black pioneer at Azusa Street, and the Alexandrian Christian tradition of Origen *(praktike, theorike, gnosis)* and others in the matters of justification, sanctification, and baptism in the Holy Spirit.[51] This scheme is typical of, say, the vision of St. Isaac, the Syrian, who distinguished three stages in the way of union: penitence, purification, and perfection.[52] The same applies to two other Pentecostal pioneers, namely Minnie Abrahams and Thomas Barrett. In fact, Abrahams describes the goal of life as "union with God," which is not unlike both the Orthodox and Luther's traditions. Furthermore, she understands the Christian life as spiritual warfare "which is best waged in prayer and ascetic lifestyle" where one is able to surrender one's self completely to the conformity of the will of God. Only through the grace of God's Holy Spirit living through the individual can the individual be successful in this personal renewal. Using language resembling that of the patristic/Orthodox tradition, Abrahams says that the individual who experiences the infusion of the Holy Spirit can fall away through lack of conformity to God's will. The journey to "union" is developmental, from stage to stage.

Significantly enough, echoing Luther's language of participation in Christ's cross, Abrahams speaks about being made perfect through conformity to Christ's death and resurrection. She also speaks about the "abiding presence of the fire of the Holy Ghost" in the hearts of those praying and fighting to be conformed to God's image.[53] According to T. Barrett, the same principles of spiritual life operate: through prayer and perfect submission to the will of God, grace is given by the Holy Spirit for the victorious life. The goals of this life are power for service and being "in Him, lost in Him and His love."[54]

One of the common ties between Eastern Orthodoxy and Pentecostalism is the emphasis on the Spirit's role in one's salvation and

[50] Ibid., 21.

[51] David Bundy, "Visions of Sanctification: Themes of Orthodoxy in the Methodist, Holiness and Pentecostal Traditions" (paper read at the European Pentecostal-Charismatic Research Association meeting, Prague, August 1997) 17–18.

[52] Vladimir Lossky, *The Mystical Theology of the Eastern Church* (Crestwood, N.Y.: St. Vladimir's Seminary Press, 1976) 204.

[53] Bundy, op. cit., 18.

[54] Ibid., 19–20, with references to original sources.

Christian walk. Pentecostals have become famous for their distinctive catchword, "Spirit-baptism." Spirit-baptism is depicted as empowerment for service and witness. The Spirit is also the key to sanctification and victorious Christian living.[55] Eastern Orthodox soteriology, as was noted in chapter 3, is totally imbued by pneumatological orientations, though never at the expense of Christology or the Trinity. For Orthodox theology, the incarnation of Christ, which took place in the power of the Spirit, is the defining theological principle. Even Pentecostal theology and spirituality—contrary to the common claims of outsiders—is not pneumatocentric, even though the idea of incarnation is not so central. Pentecostal spirituality is shaped by Christ-centeredness. Jesus Christ is depicted as the Justifier, Sanctifier, Healer of the Body, Baptizer with the Holy Spirit, and Soon Coming King. This is the classical "five-fold" gospel, or as it is sometimes known by Pentecostals, the "Full Gospel."[56] However, whereas Christ is the basis for the believer's justification and sanctification, the Holy Spirit is the person of the Trinity who draws the believer to—and makes the believer become like—Christ in the process of progressive sanctification.

Still another common denominator is the synergistic nature of both Orthodox and Pentecostal soteriologies. Not only with regard to sanctification but also justification, Pentecostals argue, not unlike the Orthodox, that God always works in line with the human will. For the Orthodox, freedom (of will) belongs to the ontological constitution of the human being; for the Pentecostals, the human being without a real capacity for choosing means resorting to a dead ritualism. In the Wesleyan spirit, "Whereas God will not save a man without his faith and assent, He absolutely cannot transform him without his continued faith and assent."[57] The New Testament scholar James Dunn has argued that there is a distinctive emphasis to three major Christian traditions: Catholic, Protestant, and Pentecostal. The Catholic church tends to subordinate the Holy Spirit to the church and its structures. Protestants tend to subordinate the Spirit to the Bible and word. The Pentecostals maintain

[55] See further, "Implications of Eastern Christian Pneumatology for Western Pentecostal Doctrine and Practice," in *Experiences of the Spirit: Conference on Pentecostal and Charismatic Research in Europe at Utrecht University, 1989*, Studies in the Intercultural History of Christianity 68 (Frankfurt am Main: Peter Lang, 1991) 23–34.

[56] See further, Kärkkäinen, *Spiritus ubi vult spirat: Pneumatology in Roman Catholic-Pentecostal Dialogue 1972–1989*, Schriften der Luther-Agricola-Gesellschaft 42 (Helsinki: Luther-Agricola-Society, 1998) 49–52 especially.

[57] Rybarczyk, op. cit., 310–11.

a much more dynamic view of the Holy Spirit's work: the Spirit is free to use any means at his disposal.[58]

Where do Orthodox fit in this scheme, which, of course, like any other generalization is nothing more than a generalization? On the one hand, Orthodox theology invests a lot in the freedom of the Spirit and treats church structures, especially universal structures, as secondary; on the other hand, Orthodoxy firmly believes that in its liturgical and sacramental life the Holy Spirit is free to operate. Yes, the word of God is highly honored, almost venerated, but the Spirit is never seen as "captive" to either written or spoken word. Edmund Rybarczyk is right in insisting that the notion of the Spirit's sovereignty is one shared by both Orthodox and Pentecostals. "Orthodoxy has historically been characterized by the conviction that God, through the person of the Holy Spirit, yearns to have intimate, existential, and mystical fellowship with His supreme creations, human beings."[59] Rybarczyk summarizes his extensive study with these comments:

> these two Traditions emphasize a personal encounter with God that not only does not find mystical-existential manifestations embarrassing, both see them as normal and necessary. Indeed, as the two express it, to allow Christ's Spirit to transform the depths of one's being will necessitate mysterious and nearly inexpressible experiences. Moreover, one may fairly aver that both Traditions are nearly magnetic in their mystical-existential pull because of their understanding of the divine-human relationship as an acutely inter-personal dynamic. Put differently, the two are as spiritually dynamic as they are because each—within its own meta-context— has developed ways to facilitate an experience of the mystery and transcendence of the infinite God. Each present that mystery in ways that draw human persons to Christ: the Orthodox through aesthetics, the Pentecostals through kinesthetics. Both emphasize that the human person was created for a transforming fellowship with God.[60]

Having delineated all these apparent similarities between Orthodox and Pentecostal theologies, one has to add a couple of words of warning. First, there is no clear historical connection between Eastern Orthodoxy and Pentecostalism; even if John Wesley's and other Holiness spiritualists' influences are given due respect as mediators of some Orthodox influences to Pentecostalism, this observation still holds.

---

[58] James D. G. Dunn, *Baptism in the Holy Spirit* (London: SCM Press, 1970) 224–45.
[59] Rybarczyk, op. cit., 313.
[60] Ibid., 422–23.

Second, with all of their similarities there is no denying the multitude of differences. To give an obvious example, Orthodox theology in general, and soteriology and ecclesiology in particular, is sacramental; Pentecostals eschew sacraments as means of grace since they believe that would diminish human freedom. To take another obvious case, Orthodox churches are episcopal even with their focus on the local churches; while there are some Pentecostal churches with bishops, no Pentecostal ecclesiologies to my knowledge are episcopal in the theological meaning of the term, which holds that for the church to be church there has to be a bishop in historic succession.

As an ecumenical epilogue to this section on Orthodox-Pentecostal perspectives on union, it is interesting to take a brief look at another ecumenical exchange that Pentecostals have had recently. Since 1972, Pentecostals have carried on an international dialogue with the Roman Catholic Church. Quite little-known even in professional ecumenical circles, that dialogue between the two largest Christian churches currently, which together constitute almost two-thirds of all Christians in the world, mainly focused on topics related to pneumatology. The topic of salvation was extensively studied together, but its profile is dramatically different from most other ecumenical talks on soteriology.[61] Whereas in the Roman Catholic-Lutheran conversations the topic of justification dominated not only the discussion on salvation but the whole dialogue, in the dialogue with Pentecostals, Roman Catholics hardly mentioned the topic! In fact, the three substantial final reports with more than one hundred pages show that the term justification does not even occur once in the text. However, the terms "salvation," "Spirit," "sanctification," and "Spirit-baptism," abound. The approach to salvation was governed by pneumatological orientations: Christian life was defined as "fullness of life in the Spirit."

Notwithstanding serious disagreements concerning soteriology (for example, the understanding of sacraments), both Catholics and Pentecostals mutually agreed that the essence of faith is "fullness of life in the Spirit" or the "indwelling of the Spirit in individuals." The common statement uses "union" language in a pneumatological framework:

> The Holy Spirit, being the agent of regeneration, is given in Christian initiation, not as a commodity but as he who unites us with Christ and the Father in a personal relationship. Being a Christian includes the recep-

[61] For a detailed discussion with documentation, see my *Spiritus ubi vult spirat*, part III "Spirit and Salvation"; see n. 56 in this chapter.

tion of grace through the Holy Spirit for one's own sanctification as well as gifts to be ministered to others.[62]

It is noteworthy that the statement sees the role of grace both in relation to one's own growth *(gratia gratum faciens)* and to others' growth *(gratia gratis data)*. It is the Spirit of Christ who unites the believer to Christ and to his people. The grace to save us from the power of sin and death is given through the Holy Spirit. Following Karl Rahner, it can be said that grace is first and foremost God's self-communication and presence through his Spirit to human existence.[63]

[62] *Final Report* of The Dialogue between the Secretariat for Promoting Christian Unity of the Roman Catholic Church and the Leaders of Some Pentecostal Churches and Participants in the Charismatic Movement within Protestant and Anglican Churches, 1972–1976 [*Information Service* 32 (1976) 32–37] #18.

[63] For details, see my *Spiritus ubi vult spirat*, 155–66, especially 160–61. For Rahner's basic idea, see his *Foundations of Christian Faith* (New York: Crossroads, 1982) 116–26.

7

One with God:
In Search of a Consensual View of Salvation

1. The Conditions and Promise of
Ecumenical Thinking about Salvation

Having surveyed widely historical and contemporary ecumenical views of salvation through the lenses of the doctrines of deification and justification, both in their classical forms as developed in the Christian East and West and in the ecumenical encounters between various churches both traditional and newer, it is time to take stock. This final chapter attempts to accomplish two things: first, the main results of our investigation will be summarized, and second, new tasks and challenges for the future thinking will be suggested.

A word of warning with regard to a search for a consensual view of salvation is in order. Ecumenical thinking does not mean collecting pieces from here and there and putting them together to make a more appealing mixture. One obvious reason for a cautious attitude is that so often major Christian doctrines in their specific denominational and/or ecclesio-cultural forms are connected with deeper underlying orientations. For example, the Eastern doctrine of deification is based on a mystical-apophatic worldview and method in theology. Also, the fact that doctrines do not emerge in a vacuum should alert us to contextual factors in shaping the form and content of Christian ideas. It is clear that the doctrine of justification in its Protestant form is shaped by the earlier Medieval feudal society with its hierarchical, judicial outlook.

As was mentioned in the introductory chapter, the existence and influence of contextual factors do not make Christian doctrines any "less"
Christian; it is inevitable that for the doctrines to make sense, they need
to relate to specific contexts, thought forms, and cultural patterns.

It has to be noted, also, that even the categories "Western" and "Eastern" are elusive. They are generalizations, and nothing more. It might
be the case that the Eastern tradition is more homogenous, whereas the
Western displays such a variety that one wonders about the legitimacy
of the term in the first place. And I am not thinking merely of the fact
that the Western camp includes both Catholic and Protestant expressions, but also that even among Protestantism there is such a variety of
orientations. However, as heuristic pointers, theological vocabulary
continues to use these terms, even though with the utmost care.[1]

With these cautions in mind, one could still pursue the challenging
line of questioning in ecumenical theology. The basic question is: Is there
something we may learn from other Christian expressions? What really
are the underlying differences? What are the potential contact points? I
agree with Paul Hinlicky who argues that "the historical-critical task of
the convergence method in ecumenical studies is largely accomplished
and that we are in a stage of reception, the results of which are not yet
fully clear."[2] If so, then the way forward lies in mutual theological experimentation,[3] to which the present study hopes to make a modest
contribution. Through experimentation and patient conversations, we
might be able to "transcend our differences of history and culture, in
order to discover the depth and breadth of the theology that does in
fact unite us," envisions the Orthodox John Breck.[4]

Ecumenical inquiry means taking language seriously and also going
beyond the recent formulations to ask whether differing language games
still have a common reference point. This was aptly noted in the Catholic-
Lutheran dialogue on justification. William Rusch pointed out that, if,
as a "metalinguistic stipulation" or "metatheological rule," the
Lutheran doctrine of justification means that all church teaching and

---

[1] Paul R. Hinlicky, "Theological Anthropology: Toward Integrating *Theosis* and Justification by Faith," *Journal of Ecumenical Studies* 34, no. 1 (Winter 1997) 44–47.

[2] Ibid., 39; see also, Harding Meyer, "The Ecumenical Dialogues: Situations-Problems-
Perspectives," *Pro Ecclesia* 3 (Winter 1994) 24–35.

[3] See further, Kenneth Paul Wesche and Paul R. Hinlicky, "Theses from Sväty Jur,"
Pro Ecclesia 4 (Summer 1995) 265–67; I am indebted to Hinlicky, "Theological Anthropology," 39 for references here.

[4] John Meyendorff and Robert Tobias, eds., *Salvation in Christ: A Lutheran-Orthodox
Dialogue* (Minneapolis: Augsburg, 1992) 106.

practices should function to promote reliance or trust in the God of Jesus
Christ alone for salvation, and that if Eastern patristic theology has done
this, whether or not it has employed the vocabulary of justification, then
from the Lutheran perspective it is "within the limits of legitimate diversity in the Christian tradition."[5]

Yet, the result of ecumenical inquiry may well be a sharpening of
differences, which is as valid a result of ecumenical exchange as is consensus or agreement. During the decades when Catholics and Lutherans
carried on conversations about the doctrine of justification and related
issues, many voices questioned whether the aim should be any kind of
consensus in the first place. Ecumenical theology should always be
open to both discovering either how different various traditions may be
or how there may be much more commonality than was believed before.

Even when a consensual view is on the horizon, differences should
not be too quickly hidden. The form of the biblical canon, which Christian
tradition believes to be divinely inspired, is a helpful reminder of the
rich plurality that should be the goal for Christian theology. The Catholic-
Lutheran joint agreement followed the principle of "unity-in-diversity":
even though a common ground was found between these two traditions, they each still cherished their own. The Catholic doctrine of justification and sanctification is still Catholic, as is the Lutheran as well.

Still, ecumenical theology and work should never be an exercise in
sterile academic talks. Encounter with other traditions challenges any
conversation partner—and it should.[6] As is well known, the Lutheran
Paul Tillich came to question whether the use of the catchword "justification by faith" is legitimate any longer, in light of the Eastern soteriology oriented to the victory of God and life over death and the demonic;
for Tillich, the Western quest for the justice of God as it was developed
by Augustine, the medieval Anselmian tradition, and later Luther and
other Reformers, no longer caught the essence of salvation.[7] On the other
hand, the Catholic Hans Küng came to the conclusion that Karl Barth's
Reformed doctrine of justification is not at all as different from the Catho-

---

[5] George Anderson, T. Austin Murphy, and Joseph A. Burgess, eds., *Justification by
Faith*, Lutherans and Catholics in Dialogue 7 (Minneapolis: Augsburg, 1985) 133.

[6] For a recent call for "challenging ecumenism," see Carl E. Braaten, "Lutherans and
Catholics Together—What's Next," *Pro Ecclesia* 7, no. 1 (1998) 7: "The point is: ecumenism
is not meant to keep things the way they are. Ecumenism calls for conversion of mind
and change of heart, and then other changes are bound to follow."

[7] Paul Tillich, *Systematic Theology*, vol. 3 (Chicago: University Press, 1967) 227; see
also vol. 2, 178.

lic as had been assumed earlier.[8] Often, what emerges out of serious ecumenical talks and study of rich Christian traditions is a changed Orthodox, Lutheran, Methodist, Episcopalian theology. This also necessarily means healthy self-criticism. Conversation with another theological tradition helps clarify one's own views and make oneself more critical toward one's own convictions.

The thesis of this study is that amidst all the differences between the East and West, the pluralism of which has come to be expressed with the help of these two doctrines, namely deification and justification, a dominant motif can be found: union with God. In fact, a further tentative proposal was made—even though the present study did not have a chance to pursue the question in any systematic way—that the idea of union is also the dominant motif of all religions.

2. Union as the Defining Motif in Eastern and Western Soteriologies

In this study, an investigation was made as to how the idea of union has been expressed in various Christian traditions in the East and West. During the course of our study it has become evident that, in fact, even though the Western theology of salvation in general and the Reformation doctrine of justification in particular have usually been interpreted as antagonistic to the Eastern doctrine of deification, in a legitimate strand of Reformation theology the idea of union is a controlling idea. It also became evident that there is a built-in tension in Reformation theology between two differing, and to some extent, conflicting views of justification, namely, the forensic view of the Lutheran confessions and the effective view of Luther's own theology. Historically, the former gained ascendancy over Luther's own views, and not until the latest renaissance of Luther studies especially in Scandinavia has it been rediscovered.

The rediscovery of the idea of union and the underlying idea of justification as an effective change of the believer have also opened up new horizons for a more consensual understanding of the classical Roman Catholic doctrine of justification and sanctification by the Reformation traditions. With all their differences, the Roman Catholic and Orthodox soteriologies have insisted on justification/deification as a

[8] Hans Küng, *Justification: The Doctrine of Karl Barth and a Catholic Response* (London: SPCK, 1964).

process of change in the human person, rather than merely a change of status or forgiveness of sins.

Our investigation also demonstrated that post-Reformation Western theology continues and sharpens that strand of Reformation theology, especially of Luther's, that tends toward an effective, dynamic view of salvation, the leading idea of which is the inner change of the person. Common to all of these later Protestant soteriologies has been the idea of salvation as radical change leading to discipleship and holiness. These traditions—Anabaptism, Methodism, and Pentecostalism—with all of their differences, have insisted on the need for sanctification as a necessary and integral part of the process of salvation. One wonders if the membership of these and similar revivalist movements in the Protestant family of churches is more a result of historical coincidence than theological choice. For example, the Radical Reformation Anabaptism shares in its doctrine of justification more similarities with Roman Catholicism than with Lutheranism, even though their doctrine came to be expressed with the help of Reformation conceptual apparatus. The same can be said, for example, of early Methodism. Its burning desire to attain union with God by turning away from all known sin and its uncompromising call for discipleship leans naturally toward Catholic mysticism and monastic traditions. It also has surprising similarities with the asceticism and spiritual vision of the Christian East.

What has been groundbreaking in this study is the fact that the doctrine of salvation, which traditionally has been the hallmark of church divisions not only between the East and West but also between Western Catholic and Protestant traditions, has the potential of serving as a bridge between the East and West, between Catholics and Protestants, and finally, between the older and younger churches. One of the deficiencies of ecumenical theology has been its overlooking or minimizing the contribution and challenge of younger churches, Baptists, Methodists, Mennonites, Pentecostals, and numerous independent churches. Yet the future of the Christian church, and consequently of theology, lies to a large extent in the developments in these traditions.[9]

---

[9] See further: Miroslav Volf, *After Our Likeness: The Church as an Image of the Trinity* (Grand Rapids: Eerdmans, 1998) 12–13 especially; Russell Chandler, *Racing Toward 2001: The Forces Shaping America's Religious Future* (Grand Rapids: Zondervan, 1992); 210ff. Even the conservative prefect of the Vatican's doctrinal office has admitted that the future of the Christian church lies predominantly in the developments of various Free Churches; Joseph Cardinal Ratzinger, *The Ratzinger Report: An Exclusive Interview on the State of the Church: Joseph Cardinal Ratzinger with Vittorio Messori* (San Francisco: Ignatius, 1985) 46.

Linked with the main result of this study, several corollary issues related to a consensual view of salvation in the Eastern and Western theologies emerged in this inquiry. The main perspectives could be summarized in five theses; each of these perspectives will be discussed in detail in the following:

1. New Testament studies have radically challenged the classical understanding of justification.

2. Sanctification and inner change form an integral part of the doctrine of justification and cannot be distinguished from each other.

3. The category of love belongs to the essence of justification/deification and cannot be set in antithesis with faith.

4. The question of the freedom of the will in salvation has to be studied afresh.

5. The doctrine of salvation cannot be expressed only in Christological terms but requires pneumatological grounding as well.

3. Fresh Voices from the Bible

According to both the Lutheran-Orthodox and Lutheran-Catholic dialogues on salvation, the return to the language and teaching of the Bible has opened up new vistas for a conciliar understanding of the doctrine of salvation.[10] At the same time, more recent biblical studies have also seriously questioned the centuries-long established canons of interpretation, especially with regard to the doctrine of justification. On the basis of these considerations, some have questioned whether the catchword "justification by faith" is legitimate anymore.

The new ecumenical thinking about justification and salvation needs to take stock of the main results of recent biblical inquiry. Notwithstanding the continuing debate and unresolved state of many issues, several biblical perspectives on the issue of justification are becoming established as the mainline stance. Since justification is one of many legitimate images of salvation in the Bible, it cannot be made *the* hermeneutical key.

---

[10] Meyendorff and Tobias, eds., op. cit., 24: "Both traditions have continued to employ the language of the Bible as the primary vehicle of theological expression and spiritual understanding"; Lutheran World Federation and the Roman Catholic Church, *Joint Declaration on the Doctrine of Justification* (Grand Rapids, Mich.: Eerdmans, 2000) #8: "Our common way of listening to the word of God in Scripture has led to . . . new insights."

Justification is but one window into the rich biblical imagery of salvation. Terms such as redemption, forgiveness, atonement, reconciliation, adoption, overcoming death, making peace, and a host of others have to be given, if not equal then at least, proper voice. The plurality of approaches to the doctrine of salvation in the Bible should alert us to the danger of trying to single out one and put it above the others. In addition, the hermeneutical role of the doctrine of justification has to be restudied. Luther's "canon within the canon" approach, based on the critical role of the doctrine of justification by faith, is an arbitrary, extra-biblical hermeneutical rule that does not do justice to the richness of biblical revelation.

The great advantage of cherishing the multifaceted biblical view of salvation is that it helps us connect with various needs in human life. For example, in some Asian contexts (like Japan), guilt (and the needed forgiveness) is not the main category of human-divine or human-human relationships, but rather shame; consequently, the purpose of salvation is to deal with shame and related issues.[11] A whole variety of issues in human life and society have direct soteriological implications, such as the need for liberation and the quest for the value of life.

Scholarship agrees that the term *righteousness* in the Bible refers to the righteousness that is God's own characteristic. God is just, righteous in all of his dealings. Righteousness with regard to human being means, then, primarily being in consonance with God's own character. The terminology of "imputation of righteousness" that can occasionally be found in some Pauline passages in the New Testament is a derivative concept and merely one way to illustrate dimensions of salvation.

If *righteousness* refers primarily to God's own righteous character, then it means that the distinction between *justification* and *sanctification*, while possible theologically, cannot be supported by biblical data. To be righteous means making just, setting a person in a right relationship with God and with others. Even when justification requires individual response, it is not merely individualistic; it is integrally related to God's saving purposes for the covenant community and to the coming of the kingdom of God. Righteousness is a relational concept and has implications for both divine-human and human-human relationships, as will become evident in the following discussion.

What about the meaning of *deification*? What is the biblical approach to this Eastern concept? Scholarship agrees that the term *theosis* is rare

---

[11] For a fine treatment of shame from a christological and soteriological perspective, see the book by the Mennonite C. Norman Kraus, *Jesus Christ Our Lord: Christology from a Disciple's Perspective* (Scottdale, Penn.: Herald Press, 1987) 204–17.

in the biblical canon. The claim of the Eastern theological tradition for the prominence of the *idea* of deification in the Bible might be valid, but it is simply a fact that terminological attestation is scarce. Thus, determining the biblical status of the idea of deification requires a search for other terminology that carries the same meaning. Terminology related to union is a central biblical category with the rich occurrence of expressions such as "in Christ" and "with Christ."

Unfortunately, the Eastern church has not been active in pursuing critical biblical studies on the concept of salvation, and if they have, they are not easily available to the theological guild. At this point, we simply lack reliable biblical studies. The Eastern theologians' supporting of their claim for the extensive biblical attestation of the idea of deification is more guided by apologetic concerns than theological accuracy. One wonders whether any kind of reappraisal of the doctrine of deification will happen when critical studies on the concept of deification emerge, in a way parallel to what is happening to the concept of justification by faith.

4. "Be Holy as I Am Holy"

The biblical tradition, both in the Old Testament and in the New, approaches the question of salvation from the perspective of the likeness of God's people to God. In other words, to be saved means becoming like God. In order for this to happen, a change has to take place in the human person. Of course, this may entail a change of status, as if somebody who has committed a crime is being pardoned. This, however, is not the main direction of the biblical data. Thus, the Catholic and Eastern traditions as well as post-Reformation Free Church traditions, in line with the Radical Reformation, have always challenged the magisterial Reformation with neglecting this biblical data.

The Eastern doctrine of deification, the Catholic doctrine of justification, as well as the Anabaptist and Methodist theologies have maintained the inner logic between justification and sanctification as integral parts of salvation. Inner change and change of status cannot be distinguished from each other. The doctrine of sanctification has turned out to be one of the most painful dividing issues in the Lutheran versus Catholic and Orthodox conversations on salvation and also within Protestantism between magisterial and radical Reformation traditions. Ironically, the Lutheran tradition has come to be known as one that supports "bold sinning." As the Lutheran Hinlicky pointedly notes,

"Justification by faith easily becomes an abstract declaration of divine permissiveness that leaves secularized persons to work out their own spiritual ruin with a foolishly happy conscience."[12]

One may wonder why the forensic view of justification has gained prominence in Reformation theology. The obvious reason is that the Reformation doctrine emerged as a reaction to what was once considered the excesses of the Catholic view. Reactionary views are always one-sided; even when they appropriately respond to the crises of their times, as soon as they become consolidated and established as part of a tradition, they usually lead towards a biased understanding. On the other hand, the classic Catholic view as expressed at the Council of Trent also tended to be biased: in its fear of neglecting the need for change in the person, its rejection of the value of the forensic view contributed to an unfortunate division.

One also wonders whether the difficulty in the Western church, especially among the Reformation traditions, to listen carefully to the passionate appeal of the Eastern church for a necessary change of the human person as a result of growing into Christ-likeness has been hampered by the term "deification" itself, apart from its strict meaning. As ancient as the term is, it has always been looked at with some suspicion. Many Westerners have wondered whether it borders on idolatry or some physical understanding of spirituality not unlike Catholic theology's view of sacramental transubstantiation. Of course, the Eastern emphasis on a more positive anthropology and distinctive definition of sin and its results have also made their Western counterparts less willing to hear about sanctification as an integral part of salvation. One also wonders whether Martin Luther's "canon within the canon" principle which elevated the term *justification* as the highest critical norm of Christian revelation, made Reformation churches too anxious to take count of the term *justification/righteousness* in determining the orthodoxy of any theological position. For the Eastern church, the term is almost unknown, even though the idea is not.

Nevertheless, the discovery of Martin Luther's own theology of justification with its insistence on the inner change of the person as the result of Christ's presence in the believer not only challenges Lutheran

[12] Hinlicky, "Theological Anthropology," 41; according to Hinlicky, "For abundant contemporary evidence of Lutheran reasoning in the form, 'let us sin that grace may abound,' see "A Collection of Responses from ELCA Academicians and Synodical Bishops to *The Church and Human Sexuality: A Lutheran Perspective*, First Draft of an ELCA Social Statement" (Chicago, 1994).

tradition with all of its built-in tensions, but also opens up the question of love and good deeds in a fresh way.

5. Loving in Faith

Luther is usually looked upon as the theologian of justification by faith, and rightly so. A less-known aspect of his work has been the prominence of the idea of love as the structuring principle of his theology. Luther's creative correlation between the theology of the cross and theology of love, both divine and human, have opened up fresh avenues for Western theology to relate the relationship with God to other people. Luther was clear about the priority of God's love. As a result of justification, God's love in the form of Christ's real presence is given to the believer and consequently, she begins to act as Christ would have acted. Rather than seeking her own benefits, the Christian loves other people and the world with a divine kind of love that creates its objects rather than assesses their value on the basis of their characteristics. As we found out, this kind of theology of love necessarily has implications for the doctrine of the church: the church becomes a hospital for the sick. Even when the church still betrays unfortunate human characteristics, such as competition and lack of care, Christians guided by the living Christ in their heart are moved to reach out to those in need of help.

Luther's theology of love, naturally, also opens up new possibilities for approaching the painfully dividing question of the role of good works with regard to salvation. Luther was clear about the nature of salvation as a free gift. He was also clear about the essential link between receiving Christ's presence through faith and its irresistible power in beginning the renewing work to make the believer become more Christlike, equipped to do good works. It is understandable that the Lutheran confessions never satisfactorily solved the question of good works with regard to salvation, especially given the highly polemical nature of the documents. A forensic view of justification, at its best, makes good works more or less optional; what matters is the legal exchange of status whether good works do or do not follow.

The category of love has always been more prominent in the theologies of both the Eastern church and the Catholic church. This has been the result of two theological guidelines. On the one hand, both the Orthodox and Catholic traditions, with reference to Romans 5:5 and similar passages, have believed that in justification/deification the love of God has been poured out into the believer's heart through the Holy

Spirit. On the other hand, both traditions have also emphasized the role of good deeds as a natural and necessary human result of what God has done. They share the conviction that if good deeds are lacking there is a serious reason to doubt whether an inner change has taken place at all. To many Protestants this has bordered on human merit, but neither Eastern nor Catholic tradition has understood it that way; their point of reference has been the biblical idea of a healthy tree producing good fruit. The Radical Reformation and post-Reformation movements similarly have insisted on the need for neighbor love and good deeds as a sign of being a Christian. For example, the small Anabaptist congregations took literally the example of the early church to divide their possessions, care about the needy among them, and reach out to the world in self-sacrificing love.

There is no doubt that in biblical theology, faith and love are integrally correlated. While the Reformation era Catholic-Protestant disputes are understandable against the historical background, they have little to do with the consistent biblical insistence that mere profession of faith without love is self-deceiving. It simply is the fact that the biblical emphasis on "faith alone" is never meant to be read in a way that makes good works insignificant. The church catholic from the beginning has struggled with how to keep the balance between the totally unmerited gift of salvation and the equally important role of love and good works; this tension, however, is to be maintained rather than seen as a threat to the gospel of grace. This question relates to the topic of free will, to which we turn next.

6. Free to Sin or Free to Become Like God?

One of the most divisive issues between the East and West has been the problem of human freedom with regard to salvation. All theological traditions agree on two premises: on the one hand, human beings are given relative freedom as a result of being created in God's image; on the other hand, human freedom at its best is relative, since human beings are not autonomous and their use of will is marred by the existence of sin. Divergences begin here. Eastern Orthodox theology insists on the freedom of will, and Catholic theology basically agrees, as do most post-Reformation theologies such as Methodism and Pentecostalism. Orthodox theology regards freedom as belonging to the constitution of human beings.[13] The

[13] Risto Saarinen, "Salvation in the Lutheran-Orthodox Dialogue: A Comparative Perspective," *Pro Ecclesia* 5 (1996) 204.

Lutheran doctrine, in its vehement opposition to what it saw as the pitfall of the Catholic view, practically speaking came to deny the whole concept of human freedom with regard to salvation. Reformation theologians have also accused Eastern Orthodoxy of two cardinal errors: free will and *synergia*. Interestingly enough, the same accusations are usually leveled against Free Church soteriologies. For example, Pentecostal sources freely speak about the role of the human will.[14] According to Rybarczyk, the Pentecostal doctrine of sanctification "is clearly synergistic." But he adds that the synergistic pneumatological-anthropological position is based on the belief that "the Holy Spirit is sovereignly free to interact with the believer on an individual basis."[15]

So, there is quite a wide gap between those views that regard freedom as either necessary for any talk about human responsibility or belonging to the human constitution and those that regard freedom merely as the capacity to sin. Can anything constructive be said at this point of ecumenical developments?

The background to the alleged impasse may be found in the (pre)Reformation debates concerning the relationship between nature and grace. The Methodist Lyle Dabney,[16] who teaches in a Catholic theological school, has identified two different models of doing theology. The oldest model he calls the theology of "the first article." It is the scholastic Thomastic model that finds its point of departure in the goodness— although not of course, in the sinlessness—of God's creation. The basic axiom of this type of theology is that grace fulfills that which is in nature: "Grace does not destroy, but rather presupposes and perfects nature."[17] Over and against this claim stands the theology of the sixteenth-century Reformation that is based on the second article (Christology), and assumes discontinuity rather than continuity between nature and grace. From Luther to Barth there are various nuances but the

[14] David Bundy, "Visions of Sanctification: Themes of Orthodoxy in the Methodist, Holiness and Pentecostal Traditions" (paper read at the European Pentecostal-Charismatic Research Association meeting, Prague, August 1997) 17, 20.

[15] Edmund Rybarczyk, *Beyond Salvation: An Analysis of the Doctrine of Christian Transformation Comparing Eastern Orthodoxy with Classical Pentecostalism* (Ph.D. dissertation, Fuller Theological Seminary, 1999) 311.

[16] Lyle Dabney, "Why Should the Last Be First? unpublished lecture at a seminar on "An Advent of the Spirit: Orientations in Pneumatology," held at Marquette University April 17–19, 1998. For further details, see Lyle Dabney, *Die Kenosis des Geistes: Kontinuität zwischen Schöpfung und Erlösung in Werk des Heiligen Geistes* (Neukirchen-Vlyun: Neukirchener Verlag, 1997).

[17] *"Gratia non destruit, sed supponit et perficit naturam."* The classic locus of this axiom is in Thomas Aquinas, *Summa Theologica* 1a.1.8.

same kind of insistence on the incompatibility of human nature and God's grace.

Now, Free Church soteriology has traditionally identified itself with the Reformation camp in its fear of Catholicism and their "work-based" view of salvation. Orthodox tradition does not easily fit either category; it does not operate at all along the lines of a nature-grace opposition. Ironically, both Orthodox and Free Church views, though, seem to be on the same side, so to speak. For neither tradition is there any denying the relative freedom of human will and responsibility, although Free Churches often have not acknowledged the tension in relation to the strict Lutheran view of human beings as almost as inactive as a "stone or log of wood."

As a way out of the old dichotomy, Dabney suggests a theology "of the third article," which finds its orientation in the doctrine of the Holy Spirit. It represents "continuity through discontinuity which begins its witness to Christ with the Holy Spirit, is rooted in the Trinitarian event of the cross, and then defines the Christian community in those categories."[18] A pneumatological concept of grace, anchored in the cross of Christ and a trinitarian vision, might help to reassess the traditional dilemma.

Eastern Orthodox tradition might be helpful here with its insistence on pneumatological orientations on the one hand, and on the need for divine human *synergy*, on the other. This enterprise might, of course, border on Pelagian charges; Orthodox theology, however, does not regard itself as (semi)Pelagian,[19] but insists on a different kind of anthropology and a legitimate divine-human *synergy*. It seems to me, for example, that Free Churches have been so eager to identify themselves with the Reformation doctrine of justification[20] that they have not seen how much their anthropology and view of human responsibility is at variance with the traditional Reformation view. The openness to an enhanced role of the Spirit in salvation may reveal new vistas for a more balanced soteriology.

[18] Dabney, op. cit., 19.

[19] I am indebted to Fredrik Cleve, "Samtalen mellan Finlands och Rysslands kyrka," in *Nordisk Ekumenisk Årsbok 1978–1979* (Helsinki: Kirkkohallitus, 1980) 84; and Risto Saarinen, *Johdatus ekumeniikkaan* ["Introduction to Ecumenics"], (Helsinki: Kirjaneliö, 1994) 158.

[20] E.g., Finnish Pentecostal Churches issued a formal statement about the Roman Catholic-Lutheran *Joint Declaration on the Doctrine of Justification* in which the Pentecostals emphasized the forensic understanding of justification, "Kannanotto vanhurskaut-tamisjulistukseen" [A Statement on Joint Declaration on Justification"] (unpublished).

7. Toward a Pneumatological Doctrine of Salvation

One of the main differences between Eastern and Western theologies has been the prominence of a pneumatological outlook in the East. As a result, as we noticed in chapter 3, the Eastern doctrine of salvation has come to be expressed in balanced pneumato-christological terms. The Reformation doctrine of salvation is open to pneumatological perspectives even though it easily lends itself primarily to christological categories. The rediscovery of Martin Luther's own theology with the idea of Christ's presence in the believer through the Holy Spirit as the justification of the human person opens up a new appreciation of the role of the Spirit in salvation.

The doctrine of salvation cannot be expressed in christological terms alone but requires pneumatological grounding as well. The Reformed Jürgen Moltmann has a helpful section on soteriology in his *Spirit of Life* where he criticizes the traditional Reformation/Lutheran view for not paying due attention to the role of the Spirit in salvation. Referring to passages like Titus 3:5-7, which speaks about the "washing of regeneration and renewal in the Holy Spirit, which he poured out upon us richly," Moltmann emphasizes that "'regeneration' as 'renewal' comes about through the Holy Spirit" when the "Spirit is 'poured out.'"[21] By making further reference to John 4:14, the metaphor of the divine "well-spring of life" which begins to flow in a human being, he contends that "through this experience of the Spirit, who comes upon us from the Father through the Son, we become 'justified through grace.'"[22]

Moltmann contends that "in order to present regeneration of men and women as their justification, the Reformation doctrine of justification has to be expanded" in three interrelated directions. First, it must show the saving significance of Christ's death and resurrection. Second, it must from the outset be presented pneumatologically as the experience of the Spirit. And, third, it must be eschatologically oriented.[23]

Moltmann's emphasis helps us to reorient soteriology toward a proper pneumatological balance. First, it focuses on the crucial role of the Spirit in justification and regeneration in accordance with many New Testament witnesses. Second, it puts more stress on the process of sanctification than traditional Reformation doctrine has done. Again,

[21] Jürgen Moltmann, *Spirit of Life: A Universal Affirmation*, Margaret Kohl, trans. (Minneapolis: Fortress, 1992) 146.

[22] Ibid.

[23] Ibid., 411; see also Kenneth L. Bakken, "Holy Spirit and Theosis: Toward a Lutheran Theology of Healing," *St. Vladimir's Theological Quarterly* 38, no. 4 (1994) 410–11.

quoting Moltmann: "The operation of the Spirit as we experience it is therefore a double one: it is the justification of the godless out of grace, and their rebirth to a living hope through their installation in their right to inherit God's future. The justification of the godless is the initial operation of the outpouring of the Spirit."[24]

Paul Hinlicky reminds us of the fact that too often Reformation theology has lost sight of its connection to Augustine's theology and imagined as going straight back to the Bible, to the Pauline idea of justification. In fact, Augustine is the father of both the Catholic and Reformation doctrine of salvation, and his soteriology is pneumatologically informed, as the recent study by M. Ruokanen, which we analyzed in chapter 4, clearly showed. For Augustine, no credit for righteousness will be given to the human being but rather to God. Yet in order for the righteousness to be genuine, a new obedience is called for, not just a "legal fiction." But it is only through "the example of Christ and by his gracious gift of the Holy Spirit [that] this achievement of righteousness has become a new possibility for believers."[25] This perspective was vital for Luther, but became sidetracked in Melanchthon's formulation of the Lutheran confessions. It is now being rediscovered. "So justifying faith is for Luther a rapture or ecstasy, a personal Pentecost."[26]

In his recent comprehensive formulation of an ecumenical Lutheran doctrine of justification, Wolfhart Pannenberg has drawn our attention to the fact that for Luther the concept of faith is really "ecstatic"; its point of reference and foundation is outside oneself.[27] This view approaches also the current Roman Catholic doctrine of grace according to which salvation is God's self-communication to humanity through the Spirit of God.[28] As such, faith is always participatory and communal, the work of the Holy Spirit. As the Roman Catholic theologian Jared Wicks succinctly states, Luther's view of faith means "the exchange with Christ outside myself":

> At the exact center of spiritual existence, according to Luther, the believer is realizing his situation as one of participation and exchange with Christ,

[24] Moltmann, *Spirit of Life*, 146–47.

[25] Hinlicky, "Theological Anthropology," 58.

[26] Ibid., 60.

[27] Wolfhart Pannenberg, *Systematic Theology*, G. W. Bromiley, trans. (Grand Rapids, Mich.: Eerdmans, 1998) vol. 3, 218, 227, et passim.

[28] This was aptly noted, e.g., in the Roman Catholic-Baptist Dialogue on salvation; see Stephen J. Duffy, "Southern Baptist and Roman Catholic Soteriologies," *Pro Ecclesia* 9, no. 4 (2000) 436.

of Christ's inhesion and cementing him to himself, and of a transforming exchange between his sin and Christ's righteousness. In "apprehending faith" I lay hold of his victory as the death of my sin and of his consummate righteousness as mine by grace. In passivity under the rapture of grace, I am taken out of my lost state into the sphere of Christ's invincible righteousness.[29]

8. "Justification in the World's Context": New Tasks for Soteriology for the Third Millennium

Even though it would be foolish to neglect the rich history of Christian tradition concerning Christian thinking about salvation, it would be equally shortsighted to be content only with past formulations of soteriology. The critical task of Christian theology is to express the living tradition in a way that not only makes sense in the present context but even points to the future.

There are several lacuna in the traditional theology of salvation that need to be addressed in light of the new challenges of the third millennium. With regard to the doctrines of deification and justification, the following two topics need to be restudied and elaborated for the Christian witness to make sense in the ever-changing world: (1) the relation of soteriology to the world's context and (2) the relation of deification and justification to other religions.

The Lutheran World Federation held a consultation in Wittenberg, Germany, October 27–31, 1998, entitled "Justification in the World's Context." The consultation set itself the task of examining the significance and relevance of the Lutheran doctrine of justification by faith with regard to impending current problems: What constitutes justification in today's performance-oriented societies? What does it signify in North American society? What is its relevance in Latin America, Asia, and Africa? What challenges confront Lutherans in an increasingly secularized Europe? How does the message of justification manifest itself in the light of global interaction? Or in relation to social injustice or to the internet? These and other questions were pondered by participants from all continents. With contributions from politics and the sciences, journalism, philosophy, and theology this event was truly interdisciplinary.[30]

[29] Jared Wicks, *Luther and His Spiritual Legacy* (Wilmington, Del.: Michael Glazier, 1983) 137; I am indebted to Hinlicky, "Theological Anthropology," 60, for this reference.

[30] The main results of this consultation are to be found in Wolfgang Grieve, ed., *Justification in the World's Context*, Documentation 45 (Geneva: The Lutheran World Federation, 2000).

The consultation took its point of departure from Luther's 1520 pamphlet on Christian freedom. That little Reformation manifesto is an inspiration also to the current struggle of "rediscovering the liberating power of the central message of justification with regard to the life of the poor," to take seriously the cries of the oppressed and those under inhuman circumstances.[31] In other words, human justice, which in itself is an expression of God's justice, cannot be reduced to the "pneumatic reality of grace, justification, faith to a mere portent," but must take some concrete form in the world of suffering and injustice. This consultation is but one recent example of the desire to connect soteriology with social, political, and cultural challenges.

Walter Altmann from Latin America has issued a call for Lutherans to expand the traditional doctrine of justification to encompass social responsibility:

> The story of Jesus, poor and rejected but still in our favor, immediately broadens the forms of Christ's works beyond the merely individualistic. . . . For Luther, passivity occurred exclusively in the relationship with God. When Luther was freed, he was freed from "doing all he could." Justification by faith is never all there is. It immediately reveals the importance of commitment to one's neighbors and to their needs.[32]

Another Latin American, Alberico Baeske, emphasizes that "Luther's faith materialized itself in his freedom."[33]

While it is true that traditionally Luther's theology of justification has been limited to one's relation to God, it also is the case that the rich potential of the Eastern doctrine of deification has not been unraveled with regard to burning issues in ecology, creation, and society. In fact, the cosmic orientation of Eastern anthropology and the communitarian emphasis of much of Eastern theology could provide unprecedented theological resources for a revived theology of creation and social concern. It is perhaps due to the more conservative and isolationist mentality of many of those cultures where the Eastern church exercises its influence that so little work in this direction has been presented to the ecumenical world. It would make a fascinating study topic and theme

---

[31] See further, Wolfgang Grieve, "The Significance of Justification in the World's Context: Towards a New Interpretation of the Doctrine of Justification," in *Justification in the World's Context*, 13–14. See also Nelson Kirst, ed., *Rethinking Luther's Theology in the Context of the Third World* (Geneva: The Lutheran World Federation, 1990).

[32] Walter Altmann, *Luther and Liberation: A Latin American Perspective*, Mary M. Solberg, trans. (Minneapolis: Fortress Press, 1992) 37.

[33] Kirst, op. cit., 33.

for ecumenical conversations to invite Lutherans and Orthodox theologians to draw from their own and one another's' wells and inquire into the cosmic, social, and political implications of their doctrines.

Interestingly enough, the left wing of the Reformation, especially the Anabaptists, have materialized more concretely in social life their insistence on salvation as discipleship. Anabaptism has championed pacifism, taken action to correct social injustice, and lived out the lifestyle of suffering and self-denying love. The Methodist call for holiness and sanctification in everyday life has often elicited world-transforming social visions and programs.

These and other similar examples give promise for the future. Ecumenical collaboration is called to expand the doctrine of salvation to encompass the whole creation. A word of warning, however, is appropriate here to avoid two obvious pitfalls. One pitfall involves soteriological terms, such as justification or deification, being uncritically appropriated with "semi-secular"[34] meanings that loosen its connection with the people of God and individuals to be saved. While retaining remnants of Christian terminology, such a secularized form of social improvement ends up being little more than wishful dreams with nothing specifically "Christian" in it. The other tendency is that the most complicated philosophical and theological relationship between individual and collective (one and many) is not analyzed and soteriological terms are in that sense uncritically applied to both dimensions. Now there is no doubt that in the Bible salvation is a much more comprehensive term than the individual's entrance to heaven from a bad and sinful world; still, questions such as "How are individual and cosmic salvation conditioned by each other?" and "What, if any, is the order of priority?" have to be carefully pondered. I have not seen much work on these issues in soteriology, whereas for example in ecclesiology many theologians have wrestled with the question.

9. Deification, Justification, and Other Religions

Any inquiry into the relevance of the doctrine of justification and deification for the current world context has to take into consideration the concerns of a theology of religion, in other words, the question as to what, if any, is the salvatory value of religions. Questions regarding

[34] When using "secular" here in a sort of pejorative sense, I am not implying the dichotomy between "holy/religious" and "secular" that has too often governed much of the theological discussion about salvation.

where salvation is to be found, the role of Christ in salvation, and the contributions of religions to salvation, occupy the center of heated discussion in a world that has brought adherents of different religions to live in the same neighborhoods.

In the opening chapter, I referred to the fact that the doctrine of deification carries with it a lot of potential with regard to a dialogue between Christian faith and other faiths, including all the emerging forms of spirituality in the West and elsewhere. Recently it has been suggested that in the African context, for instance, the Eastern Orthodox concept of *theosis* may provide a challenging encounter with the concept that has been called "vital participation." I also noted that the concept of union as expressed in the doctrine of deification not only appeals to people living amidst other Eastern religions but also to those in the West under the emerging worldview that has become extremely sensitive to divine presence and purpose and permeated by a yearning for union with the divine. The concept of *theosis,* as was also suggested in the introductory chapter, may serve as a needed contact point between the new scientific post-mechanistic outlook that opens up a more nuanced understanding of "material," an understanding in which the boundary line between "spirit/spiritual" and "matter/material" is becoming more and more elusive.

Even here, however, as Christian theologians let us not be naïve and overly optimistic. The postmodern developments of philosophy of science may perhaps sharpen the opposition to religions in general and Christianity in particular; what I am saying here is that there is *potential* contact point here. Again, it has to be confessed that because of the less expansive and more introverted nature of its spirituality, the Eastern theological guild has for the most part missed the dialogue not only to its own detriment but also to the detriment of Christian theology in general. Perhaps the time has come to join forces, both from the Christian East and West, and begin the common search. In order for the joint venture to begin, Eastern and Western Christian theologians need to talk to each other to make sure that they do have enough common foundation. Even that task in a large measure is still pending, and is a task to which the present book wants to contribute.

With regard to the doctrine of justification, some modest work has been done to address the concerns of other religions. In a recent collection of essays titled *Right With God: Justification in the Bible and the World,*[35]

---

[35] D. A. Carson, ed., *Right with God: Justification in the Bible and the World* (London: The Paternoster Press and Grand Rapids, Mich.: Baker Book House, 1992).

contributors from various contexts have also addressed the issue of the relevance of the doctrine of justification with regard to Hinduism, Islam, and Buddhism. Even though in general the tone of the book is not always so conciliar as to champion a broadly "evangelical" doctrine of justification,[36] the line of inquiry is promising. Sunand Sumithra from India reminds us of the fact that Hinduism is primarily a religion of duty. The word for "religion" in India is *dharma,* which also means "duty personified." "Hence, though the terminology of justification is not found in the index of any Hindu scriptures, yet justification would be universally understood by Hindus to mean that one stands justified before the whole of society if one has done one's duty or what is socially appropriate."[37]

On the other hand, Chris Marantika from Indonesia thinks that Islam and Christianity are totally in opposition to each other: in Islam salvation is based on good works, whereas in Christianity salvation comes by faith in the righteousness of God. However, the common denominator could be the belief in one God, who in the final analysis determines who is to be justified.[38] For Buddhism, as the Japanese Masao Uenuma argues, the whole question of the relevance of the Christian doctrine of justification is even more complicated since one may wonder if Buddhism has any concept of salvation in the first place. What is the meaning of "emptiness" or enlightenment vis-à-vis justification?[39] These and a host of other questions await those who dare to enter into dialogue with other religions from the perspective of the Christian view of salvation as deification and justification.

The task ahead of Christian theology in its attempt to express the hope of Christian salvation is twofold with regard to other religions. One is the missionary task of searching for bridge-builders. Questions such as these have from the time of the early fathers occupied the minds of Christian theologians who have wanted to communicate their faith to people of other religions and worldviews: "Is there any contact point between Christian hope and that of other religions?" "Could the idea of Christian salvation be expressed in a way that makes sense to those used to another kind of language-game?" "Are there any common pointers (or real differences) beyond the seemingly different concepts of

[36] The book is sponsored by the World Evangelical Fellowship.

[37] Sunand Sumithra, "Justification by Faith: Its Relevance in Hindu Context," in *Right With God,* 216.

[38] Chris Marantika, "Justification by Faith: Its Relevance in Islamic Context," in *Right With God,* 228.

[39] Masao Uenuma, "Justification by Faith: Its Relevance in a Buddhist Context," in *Right With God,* 243.

salvation in religions?" Even though the term "contextualization" has almost lost its dynamic force because of its uncritical and ambiguous use, that is what it is all about: to talk about Christian salvation in a way that is understandable in any given context. The obvious weakness of much of contextualization, however, has been its focus on the conceptual level and its overly optimistic hope of always finding a real common foundation. Even when two religions speak about salvation in similar terms, it might be the case that behind the conceptual similarities there are radical differences in the deep structure. Care and careful analysis should be mentors in this field rather than hasty "practicality" and a desire to develop more "effective" evangelistic tools.

This brings us to the second part of the task of Christian soteriology with regard to other religions. Christian theology has to ask the critical question of whether it can learn from an encounter with other religions. Christian theologians and preachers from the beginning have not only been teachers of the nations but also eager students. If God's revelation is to be found in all of his creation, and even with all the imperfections to be found in religions, including the way Christians themselves understand the divine truths, then the common search of humanity to find union with God may teach Christians valuable lessons. The fact that the idea of union in religions is, of course, much more pronounced than, say, the Western idea of justification, may be a call to Christians to take another look at the biblical and patristic sources and ask whether the church has been one-sided in its language about salvation. Christians should also ask the critical question of how much weight should be given to intra-Christian confessional debates vis-à-vis the rest of the world of religions. Some of the internal soteriological disputes between Christians, rather than being life-and-death questions, appear to be quite minimal in importance in contrast to the need for a theology of religions. Ignoring confessional and theological nuances does not make us better communicators of the Christian faith, but neither does the unending divisive, polemical, and apologetic attitude, which has characterized so much of Catholic-Protestant and Western-Eastern relationships, contribute to relations with adherents of other religions.

The personal confession of faith of the Lutheran Paul R. Hinlicky is ecumenically promising and points toward a more conciliar approach between various Christian traditions:

> As a Lutheran, I want to say that the Orthodox doctrine of *theosis* is simply true, that justification by faith theologically presupposes it in the same

way that Paul the Apostle reasoned by analogy from the resurrection of the dead to the justification of the sinner. Indeed, justification as a declaration of faith in Christ is unwarranted except as an anticipation of the end of history and the unambiguous coming and revelation of the reign of God. Lutherans are confused about justification today because they have neglected this presupposition, to wit, that the point of justification is to bring us into communion with God through Jesus Christ. Justification is not to be understood as a theological alternative to *theosis* (as the various secular theologies of today urge) but, rather, as a commentary about how to communicate it in the present epoch between the times. In turn, the goal and content of salvation as *theosis* and the doctrine of the Holy Spirit, which that opens up for Lutheranism, clarifies the desperately muddled understanding of the relation of justification and sanctification in modern Lutheranism.[40]

---

[40] Hinlicky, "Theological Anthropology," 63.

Index

Abrahams, Minnie, 111
African context/theology, 2, 8, 134
Althaus, Paul, 59
Altmann, Walter, 132
amor Dei and *amor hominis*. *See* love
Anabaptist, Anabaptism, 4, 67–71,
    120, 126, 133
    deification/theosis in, 68–70
    and Eastern Orthodoxy, 68–71
Anselm of Canterbury, Anselmian,
    22, 32, 118
anthropology, 6, 9, 20–23, 25, 64, 98,
    128, 132
Antola, Markku, 64
Apollonius of Tyana, 90
apopathic, 19, 116. *See also* mysticism
Aquinas, Thomas, Thomastic, 79, 127
Arius, Arian(ism), 26–27
ascetic, asceticism, 31, 68–69, 75–76,
    111, 120. *See also* monasticism
Ashanin, Charles, 72
Athanasius, Athanasian, 22–24, 26,
    29, 33, 35, 46–47, 74, 94
atonement, 76
Augustine, 11, 21–22, 31, 52, 63, 91,
    118, 130

Baeske, Alberico, 132
Balthasar, Hans Urs von, 9

baptism, water, 7, 19, 29, 33–34, 91,
    96, 101, 104–6
    Spirit. *See* Spirit-baptism
Barrett, Thomas, 111
Barth, Karl, 88, 118
Basil the Great, 17, 27, 33–35, 74
Beach, Alvin J., 70
Bernard of Clairvaux, 84
Braaten, Carl E., 4, 38
Breck, John, 117
Buddhism, 2, 135
Bultmann, Rudolf, 12–13
Bundy, David, 111

Cabasilas, Nicholas, 33
Calvin, John, 6, 62
Campbell, Ted, 76
Cappadocian fathers, 27, 35
Carson, D. A., 82
Catholic. *See* Roman Catholic
Charismatic theology, 64–65
Christology, christological, 23, 25, 29,
    36, 56, 62–63, 97–98, 112
Chrysostom, John, 22, 74
church fathers, 5, 24, 91
Clement of Alexandria, 74
Clement of Rome, 74
Clendenin, Daniel B., 8
contextualization, 8, 116–17, 136

in Eastern Orthodoxy, 20, 26–27,
    29–32
"grace" (*gratia, favor,* Christ as) and
    "gift" *(donum),* 52–53, 55–58
Greek fathers, 22, 24–27, 74, 94
Gregory of Nazianzus, 22, 26, 33–34,
    74
Gregory of Nyssa, 21–22, 26, 72

Harnack, Adolf von, 6, 14
Heidelberg Disputation, 40, 43, 50
Held, Heinz Joachim, 95
Herrmann, Rudolf, 57
Hinduism, 2, 135
Hinlicky, Paul, 117, 123, 130, 136
Hofmann, Melchior, 69
holiness (of Christian), 63, 69, 72–73,
    76–77, 89, 91–92, 97, 120, 133
Holiness Movements/traditions, 72,
    89, 110, 113
Holy Spirit, 28–29, 35, 61–66, 68–69,
    73, 77, 80, 84, 105, 110–13, 128–30
    and *theosis*/union/salvation, 26–27,
        32–36, 84, 92, 95–98. *See also*
        pneumatology
Hubmaier, Balthasar, 70
Hutterite(s), 68, 70

imago Dei, image of God, 20, 23–25,
    28, 70, 76, 78–79
imputation, forensic or legal, 14, 16,
    53–55, 57. *See also* justification,
    forensic
incarnation, 23–24, 26, 28–29, 60, 70, 95
individualism, individualist, 11–12, 16
Irenaeus, 4, 6, 21, 26, 47
Isaac, St., the Syrian, 111
Islam, 135

Jenson, Robert W., ix, 38
Jewish, Judaism, 10–12, 15–16. *See
    also* Old Testament
John of Damascus, 6, 36

Juntunen, Sammeli, 45
justification
    in connection with deification/
        theosis, 16, 46–49, 91, 96–98,
        119–20
    in contrast to deification/theosis,
        88–89, 98
    doctrine of, 4–6, 22, 75, 81, 99–102,
        107, 116, 129, 131, 133
    "effective" or effecting real change,
        51–58, 101, 104, 107, 119
    by faith, 6, 10–11, 13, 15–16, 39,
        45–46, 48–49, 56, 62, 82, 87, 89,
        101–3, 105, 118, 121, 124, 131
        "justification by faith" ques-
            tioned, 124, 137
    forensic or declarative, 37, 51–58,
        62, 82–83, 96, 98, 101, 104–5, 107,
        119, 124–25
    and Holy Spirit, 95, 98, 101–6,
        129–30, 137
    Luther's, 10–12, 39–62, 105, 124–25,
        132
    as new self-understanding, 56–57
    in New Testament, 10–16, 81–82,
        90, 104, 122
    as relational concept, 12, 16, 78, 122
    as satisfaction, 22, 102
    term itself, 124, 133

Kallistos, of Diokleia, 17
Kant, Immanuel, 56
Käsemann, Ernst, 13
kingdom (of God/Christ), 15–16, 19,
    61, 104, 122
Knox, Alexander, 76
Kretschmar, Georg, 93–94
Küng, Hans, 118

law, 14–16, 60, 60n103, 103
liberation (as aspect of salvation), 8,
    23, 95, 104, 122, 132
Logos, 25, 28–29, 33–34, 47–48